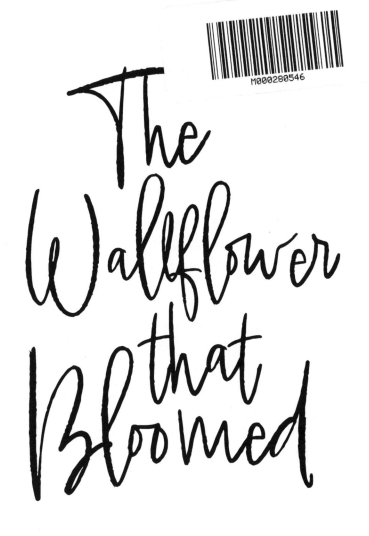

The Wallflower that Bloomed

CALLY LOGAN

BL BRIDGE
LOGOS
Newberry, FL 32669

Bridge-Logos
Newberry, FL 32669

The Wallflower That Bloomed:
Finding Your Place at the Lunch Table of Life
by Cally Logan

Printed in the United States of America

Library of Congress Catalog Card Number: 2023950090

International Standard Book Number: 978-1-61036-995-4

Edited by Lynn Copeland

Cover and interior design/layout by Ashley Morgan
GraphicGardenLLC@gmail.com

BP 3/24

*The world calls them its singers
and poets and artists and storytellers;
but they are just people who have never
forgotten the way to fairyland.*

—**L. M. Montgomery**

To my future husband:

*Something tells me you might just be a Wallflower,
and I joyously have a seat awaiting you right next to me.
Until then, my dear one.*

To Jesus Christ:

*to whom belong all praise, honor,
and glory and to whom I owe everything.*

Contents

FOREWORD........................... vii

INTRODUCTION ix

CHAPTER 1
An Invitation to the Wallflowers 1

CHAPTER 2
The Thorns 13

CHAPTER 3
Digging In 33

CHAPTER 4
Pruning 49

CHAPTER 5
The Budding 77

CHAPTER 6
The Blossoms 97

CHAPTER 7
Flowering 115

CHAPTER 8
The Blooming 131

CHAPTER 9
The Gardener 157

CHAPTER 10
Wallflowers Blooming in Real Life 169

NOTES 181

Foreword

I met Cally Logan when she was promoting her book *Dear Future Husband* and immediately was captivated. I was in awe of her perspective and her purity but most of all by her rare heart. Cally is one of those girls who is simply pure gold in thought, word, and deed. Spending an hour with Cally is like splashing through a refreshing spring on a hot summer's day.

As an older voice in the Body of Christ, I am forever on the lookout for the younger voices. I long to encourage the next generation of women who are brave enough to respond to the call of God and to reveal His fingerprint on their lives. Cally Logan is such a woman and I will be watching her life with grand anticipation.

And now that you have opened Cally's book, you get to spend hours with her. You will hear her voice, be amazed at her heart, and fall in love with her wisdom. Not only will you fall in love with Cally…but you just might fall in love with yourself in the very best way possible.

You will find yourself in this book. Cally's story, in many ways, is my story and your story. We each have a bit of our teenage soul that continues to both haunt and taunt us even in our adult years. We still quake when confronted with those among us who are richer, prettier, skinnier, or more popular than we know we will ever be. We compare ourselves to other women and always come up lacking under the self-imposed micro-scope of insecurity.

Cally's insight on these pages might have resonated with the 15-year old you but don't overlook the fact that it holds eternal wisdom for the mature you—the person you are today. With memorable quotes, engaging stories, and whimsical writing, this is a book you will be thinking about in the years to come.

The Wallflower That Bloomed is not a "one-read" book that will gather dust on your bookshelf and in your heart. The principles Cally shares, the lessons she has learned, and the loveliness of her challenging yet vibrant journey will nestle down deeply into your heart and find a life of their own there.

My prayer, as you read this book, is that you will discover who you were meant to be as never before. I hope you will throw away the results of your comparative and competitive nature and then bloom in the fullness of your individuality. I pray that your God-given gifts and childhood dreams will flourish vibrantly. Cally is just the girl to lead you, hand-in-hand with the Father on this wonderful challenge of mining for gold in your very own heart.

How wonderful to know that there are still young women like Cally who are intent on following Christ wholeheartedly! How wonderful to know that we can be a radiant demonstration of our Father's love for us.

—**CAROL MCLEOD**, Best-Selling Author and Speaker, Author of *Significant*; *StormProof*; *Guide, Guard, Grace*; *Vibrant, Joy For All Seasons* and many more.

Introduction

Those of us who are Wallflowers may feel that we adorn the walls and corners of rooms like decor, scarcely speaking more than paintings collecting dust, but that is no indication of what we have within to share, to offer, or to reflect upon. Growing up, many of us have been labeled by others (and perhaps by ourselves) as *shy, quiet, awkward, or just plain different.* We are so easily categorized and placed away that we are often glossed over without any consideration of all our worth, for we are much more than a fixture on a wall.

What if we took the stigma out of sitting at the lunch table of the outsiders? What if we stopped judging the loners, and we began to look at those around us for who they truly are? For is it not the deeply innate desire of each person to be fully known, accepted, and appreciated for the unique qualities that make them one of a kind? Furthermore, what if we did that for ourselves as well? Instead of resigning ourselves to an apathetic acceptance that we are destined for a life of solitude and judgment, we instead allowed ourselves to stand where we are—in the truth that we have been uniquely crafted by a Divine hand for such a time as this. What if we stopped fearing the judgments of others and instead bloomed into who we were always meant to be:

The Wallflower That Bloomed.

CHAPTER 1

An Invitation to the Wallflowers

I was quiet, but I was not blind.
—**Jane Austen**

*The things that make me different are
the things that make me ME.*
—**Piglet**

WHO ARE WE?

As the fifteen-year-old version of me, this is the worst part of my day: lunch period. To my chagrin my one friend, Savannah, is out today, so it looks like I'll be dining alone. A deep breath enters my lungs as I quickly spot a table in the back corner of the room that will hopefully be my hiding spot for the next forty-five minutes. So far so good, and perhaps Ashley and Emma have gotten

1

it out of their system today to beat down on me. Ashley and Emma are two of the reasons I hate coming to school and pretty much at this point loathe myself. I made the mistake last year of attempting an original style choice of a pink corduroy skirt with cute little cats embroidered on it. Rookie mistake for a freshman, even I will admit. Their sneers and comments reminded me of my place in this school and this world, and that is squarely out of sight and out of mind. When I am not being harassed for my outfit choices, they certainly find aspects of me to pick apart or exploit. Perhaps today will be different. Today we all have a test in Brit Lit, and they'll target me, but this time to use my brain. That seems to shift their tactics to be more honey and less vinegar, as they think they can bamboozle me into helping them get a good grade.

I open my meal of Campbell's Soup at Hand (seventy calories—maybe if I can finally get skinny, they'll all be nicer and more accepting) and a sugar-free store-brand Jell-O. Perfect. Also, I kept my mouth shut today as to any opinions I had in class, so there is really nothing I said that they can use against me. Sure, I don't have a North Face jacket like they do, and it is unfathomable to even dream of owning Ugg boots, but they're both kind of ugly anyhow. I am more than content in my clearance-rack Target boot-cut jeans and t-shirt from Mall of America we got last summer on our trip to see relatives. I unzip my favorite old hoodie, and eye the clock in the corner hoping lunch will go swiftly by. It doesn't.

Sure, enough Ashley and Emma make their rounds table by table as if they are campaigning or something. Man, I wish Savannah were here. I get it, she's sick or busy, or whatever, but at age fifteen I've yet to develop the maturity to not just want to cry in my Campbell's soup that my friend kind of bailed on me. Doesn't she know that she's like a lifeline here at this institution? Doesn't she know that she's the one friend I have in this world, and with things such a rollercoaster at home, having one friend makes life a little more bearable?

I try for the stiff upper lip, but I begin to shake down to my pink Converse One Stars when Emma and Ashley round the corner toward me. Why can't I just disappear? Why can't this comfort hoodie just cloak me in invisibility like Frodo's ring? They viciously shift their stare to target me next and I wilt. I'm the wallflower that wilts...

It's nearly two decades later and I can still feel the welled-up anxiety of this younger version of me. She found herself caught in the trap between wanting to fit in and desperately wanting to be accepted for who she really was. Can you relate? Are you too a Wallflower, and is it possible that instead of affixing ourselves to a wall to shrivel up and wilt we could, I dare say it, bloom?

What exactly is a Wallflower? We are those who, in a large crowd, find the center of the room to be nothing short of unpleasant. Perhaps a little gauche, these outliers find the walls of the event to be far more comfortable. Often overlooked as they are the ones outside of the bright lights, they are no less worthy. For the Wallflowers often are the dreamers, the creators, the bright-eyed wonderers of the most glorious of daydreams, and the behind-the-scenes orchestrators of some of the most beloved works of all time, the enigmatic visionaries of "to infinity and beyond." We see the world a little differently than most do, and there is nothing wrong with either lens used. I for one am an advocate of not only embracing such a position in the world, but an advocate of embracing it for all that it is in such wonderstruck glory.

What does it mean to be a Wallflower That Bloomed? It means that within there is a sincere self-acceptance no longer masking or attempting to conform to the social norms, and it is unabashedly standing confident in who you really are. Fearlessly and authentically you. Quirky, wonderful, weird, one-of-a-kind you. A person who was crafted in the image of the One True God, and someone who not only bears His thumbprint, but who has a specific purpose on this planet for this time in history. It is also a keen awareness that you will not always be everyone's cup of tea, and that is okay. What will be evident in the long run is that when you find those who truly appreciate you—not just tolerate you—your petals will thrive even more.

This leads us to the question: How can I bloom? The answer is not one that can be rolled up and easily fit into a little how-to box, but as with anything worth doing, it requires a process. So, let's set you up to bloom.

WHY WE ARE

Why are you the way that you are? If you read that in Michael Scott's voice from *The Office,* then extra gold stars on your paper today. Within every Wallflower this simple question emerges that you desperately desire to know the answer to: *why?* Why is it that there is something innately different about you? Why is it that no matter how hard you try, at some point you find yourself at a fork in the road yet again of either going along with the fake self to stay with the crowd, or taking the road less traveled where you can freely stroll as yourself. Though the road less taken is one of great freedom, it is also a lonely road. But what is it about us that makes us this way? Truth be told it's not one given answer, but to sum it up well it is that *you weren't made to be like everyone else*—and that is such a positive truth to ponder.

Ask any artist, musician, or writer and you'll hear a common phrase that at some point in their journey of life they realized they were different. They just knew it. Yet look at the goodness these difference makers bring about to this world in the way of arts, invention, and unique beauty. Consider the profound impact on human history these different individuals have made, and then take a moment to realize what a gift it is that you are one of those people. You aren't like all the others because you weren't ever meant to be. God made you to be uniquely you. To find the answer to your why, change your question from "Why am I this way?" to "What does God want me to do with these differences within me?" You have been given this one life and don't know how long it will be, so allow God to use you to leave a mark on this planet for something deeply and irrevocably beautiful. Let's keep going and embrace a little less "Why am I?" and a little more "I get to be me."

THE MASK

Most of us have a mask we keep in a jar by the door, and it's for whomever we find ourselves interacting with that day. We are profoundly dynamic creatures in our ability to shape shift into the perfectly digestible package for those we find ourselves around. Masking offers us the ability to navigate the world around us with little pushback or rejection, but what a facade of an existence.

Perhaps one of the greatest revelations of the vast variety of masks we collect for ourselves is when friends and peers from different aspects of life all come together for an event. Think of a birthday party where your old college friends, work friends, family members, and any other social groups begin to overlap, and you feel a sudden rush of anxiety with them all meeting at once. You realize that each group sees a very curated version of you that is specifically tailored to the social setting, arena, and tone appropriate for those involved. You may find that to make others more comfortable there is often a habit of "mirroring" that takes place. Mirroring is when you adopt mannerisms, phrases, and even the cadence of others and present it back to them. It is not mockery, rather it is the hope that if you reflect back to them a variant of themselves, you will be better received. Or you may fashion an easily digested portion of your personality traits so that they suit the palate of those around you, even if it is topped with artificial garnish. When multiple social groups overlap, it almost always invokes a fear of one group seeing a new side of you that you've offered to a different group. It's like when foods that you don't want to touch are mixed and you can't seem to prevent it.

But why is that? Do we really have some incriminating secret that we are trying to hide? Or are we just often insecure that once people gather different sides of us, they will become disillusioned or find us distasteful and wash their hands of us? Are we really as awful as our insecurities tell us we are? Could there exist a place where you no longer fear these groups interacting and you allow yourself to have the freedom to offer various parts and aspects of yourself authentically and fearlessly so that when these groups mingle, they all know a portion of the wonderful whole you are—not the carefully packaged version you want them to think is you?

What if you brought to the table authentic over artificial?

What if you offered a very transparent charcuterie board of yourself? Consider how many different parts of you there are and how they are all paired together in the living, breathing fullness of you. These fruits, cheeses, nuts, and meats can all exist on their own, but together they make a beautiful arrangement clearly seen as a whole, not hidden in any part. When you approach people with authenticity over artificiality you are offering that charcuterie board of delight to others. They see you as a whole with all your parts, though they may have their particular favorite parts. You no longer worry about overlapping social groups when you view yourself as a whole. The mask is not needed when you are transparent and remain consistently true to yourself, no matter who is around you.

The mask is something we can choose to keep in our back pocket to slip on, or we can make a courageous move and leave it off. Perhaps in the journey of this book you will feel inspired to leave the mask in the jar and walk out the door without it. Maybe, just maybe, you will realize that you are valuable, you are lovely, and you are who God says you are, regardless of what anyone else says. Colossians 2:10 reminds us that, "In Him you have been made complete, and He is the head over all rule and authority" (NASB95). The Greek word for "complete" means "full" in the sense that there is no longer lack. Hold firm to this truth in your journey, for if you have turned from your sin and surrendered your life to Jesus, you lack nothing in Christ. He calls you complete in Him. To quote Cinderella in the 2015 movie, "Perhaps the greatest risk any of us will ever take is to be seen as we really are." Maybe this book found its way to you because you are to take such a risk, and in doing so you will find courage, kindness, and insurmountable joy unlike you've ever known, lacking nothing. Let's attempt to slowly take off the mask, even if you are still just holding it in your hand, and let's keep moving onward into this wonderfully curious "What if I did?" kind of journey.

GARDEN PARTY

In 1971 a concert was held at Madison Square Garden in New York that changed the life of a man, and it's a story that might just change your approach toward life going forward.

Ricky Nelson was known as a teen heartthrob in the 1950s, much due to the success of his parents' hit television show, *The Adventures of Ozzie and Harriet,* where he literally grew up on screen. It was similar to shows like *Leave It to Beaver* or *I Love Lucy* in its glimpse of wholesome, sweet, 1950s suburban life. During his teen years Nelson began to sing and perform songs, and his parents quickly realized how talented their young son really was. The show began to feature Ricky singing frequently in episodes, even if the plot didn't need a musical number. Viewership rose quickly because of these on-screen performances and seemingly overnight Ricky Nelson became a household name. Many considered his talent on a par with Elvis Presley himself, though more clean-cut with less controversial dancing. In fact, in December 1958 he was featured on the cover of *Life Magazine,* where the term "teen idol" was first coined to describe him. During the '50s and '60s, his music topped the *Billboard* Hot 100 chart over fifty times, making him anything but a one-hit wonder. As the Beatles began to take over the music world, people seemed less enthralled by Ricky Nelson. This came to a head at the 1971 concert at Madison Square Garden.

Nelson was a featured guest singer, along with many other notable musicians of this time: Bo Diddley, Chuck

Berry, and Bobby Rydell. Nelson began his set with familiar hits, but as he began to play some of his new material the demeanor of the crowd shifted from praise to protest quite literally booing Nelson off the stage. They were content with his classic hits, but when he sought to share new material as the more mature style he had been cultivating, they rejected him. They wanted the plucky teenage Ricky, not the seasoned adult Ricky. Such a reaction would certainly have been a blow not just to the ego of a man, but to the integrity of an artist attempting to share his heart and art with the world around him. But the story does not end with him running off stage with his tail between his legs never to be seen or heard from again.

In 1972, Ricky Nelson released a new song he had written entitled "Garden Party," which recounted his experience at the concert the year before, but with a spin on the evening that exemplified self-acceptance and inner confidence—perhaps a reminder we could all use. The refrain of the song offers,

> It's all right now
> I learned my lesson well
> You see, you can't please everyone
> So you gotta please yourself [1]

In life, we have the choice that can only be made by our own hearts on whether we will let something make us or break us, and Nelson made the choice to let this make him. He became firm in conviction of his own personal, unique, original music and he kept sharing his gift with the world—even if the world rejected him. Ironically enough, "Garden Party" went on to be one of the greatest hits of his career, one well loved by the very generation of people who booed him off the stage. His son, Gunnar, said of his father's song,

> After a lifetime of pretending to be a character he wasn't—wearing the sweater on Monday on the set of *Ozzie and Harriet* after being a real rock star on the weekends—he was writing and performing for his own pleasure and satisfaction. The song was based on his experience at Madison Square Garden. He turned what could have remained the darkest day of his life into his brightest shining moment. Just when the music industry considered him a relic, filing him away as yesterday's news, he had the biggest hit of his career, and it was totally autobiographical.[2]

How many of us have had a similar experience where we've shared our heart with others only to face rejection? Yet we have the same choice Ricky Nelson did in the course of things, so what and where is the Garden Party of your life? And how will you take that moment or experience and find yourself making the choice to not worry about pleasing everyone? How can moments like this break the people-pleasing tendencies we fall prey to, and how can they be used to help us instead bring out something of beauty that could even inspire others in the future?

PERSONAL REFLECTION
AND APPLICATION QUESTIONS

1. What are aspects of your personality wher you would consider yourself different?

2. Who is one artist, musician, or potential Bloomed Wallflower you admire?

3. What is one way you have found yourself masking in order to help those around you feel more comfortable or pleased?

4. How would you define your own personal differences between authentic and artificial?

5. In the vein of Ricky Nelson, how could you live in such a way as to not please everyone, to stop people-pleasing?

CHAPTER 2

The Thorns

The beginning of this love is the will to let those we love be perfectly themselves, the resolution not to twist them to fit our own image. If in loving them we do not love what they are, but only their potential likeness to ourselves, then we do not love them: we only love the reflection of ourselves we find in them.
—**Thomas Merton, *No Man Is an Island***

To be yourself in a world that is constantly trying to make you something else is the greatest accomplishment.
—**Ralph Waldo Emerson**

THE WOUNDS

Soul wounds are something most all of us at some point in life experience, Wallflower or not. For some these wounds are on the surface, apparent to all. For others, you can see the wounds carried around in the eyes, which really are the gateway to the soul; and for others the wounds are carefully hidden but emerge when someone steps on the landmine that triggers it all. However these wounds are presented, they all pinpoint the deeper issue that at some time in your life something was said, done, or imposed upon your tender and formative soul that left a stain, tear, or cut that never really healed over.

In whatever way the wound was given, you—as an emotion-filled, living being—deserve to have validation. Even if the one who wounded you didn't do so intentionally, it is still your reality. Many of us have been told to "suck it up" or were gaslit to believe we are a loon for considering a comment or action as a gash, but other people are not you. Their point of view is different from yours, and yours is valid hurt harmed me." Grant yourself the permission to not just stuff it deep down or shove it under the rug. To heal the wound, you must first expose it to air. A covered laceration will not be able to fully heal unless exposed to the air, and that is true for literal and figurative wounds.

It is odd how short the teen years are in the span of a typical lifetime, but how extremely formative they are to the years that follow. As mentioned before, the thought of which lunch table we found ourselves at seems to be something many of us carry into adulthood. Numerous movies centered around the teenage years capture the situation well, even if a little hyperbolic. Take *Clueless*, for example, when the main character, Cher, is narrating all the various groups seated at lunch tables, and how even in the same groups there proved to be a lot of competition and tearing down. Even Cher's friend Tai cut her down with harsh words later in the movie. Thankfully Tai apologized, which yielded the ability to endure in friendship and the story ends happily, but it's evidence that even at the most popular table in school wounds can be caused by peers. Few of us come out of high school without something that shaped us in a new way that at first was a jarring event.

We also find examples in Scripture where individuals were belittled for "sitting at the wrong table," and we see Christ's response:

> Later, Matthew invited Jesus and his disciples to his home as dinner guests, along with many tax collectors and other disreputable sinners. But when the Pharisees saw this, they asked his disciples, "Why does your teacher eat with such scum?"
>
> When Jesus heard this, he said, "Healthy people don't need a doctor—sick people do." Then he added, "Now go and learn the meaning of this Scripture: 'I want you to show mercy, not offer sacrifices.' For I have come to call not those who think they are righteous, but those who know they are sinners." (Matthew 9:10, NLT)

Whether it occurs in their teen years or in the years that follow, people have been marginalized for eons. The Pharisees stood in judgment of Jesus for inviting those they deemed "scum" without really seeing or inquiring of the bigger reason those people had been invited in the first place.

As we attempt to remove some of the embedded thorns that have caused abrasion within us, ones that are thwarting our ability to really grow and thrive, be kind to yourself. Remember that you are the sum total of all your experiences, from infancy to this very day. Remember too that you are allowed to not be okay even decades later with how something impacted you. The key is to acknowledge the pain, expose it to the light, and work toward healing it so that it is no longer something that could hinder you from fulfilling all your potential. As we move onward, you may be reminded of one or more wounds that had an impact on who you are today, and some of those wounds may be unnerving to recall. It may be wise to keep a list of these memories, events, or recollections to air out for healing through prayer or therapy or to dissect with someone you trust. Part of healing a wound is getting out the dirt, the disease, and the infection within, and that can sting. But keep going. Remember, we are on a mission of blooming, so be kind and patient with yourself in that process; it may not be swift.

NOT ENOUGH

"I'm not enough" is something so many Wallflowers have felt at one time or another, in desiring acceptance from others, in seeking to perform well in a certain context, or just regarding life in general. What if it is not that you are not enough, but rather you are using scales and measures that are not an appropriate assessment?

We are all such different creatures, and if we judge the worth of all things using the same measure, it is not a correct or fair evaluation. That is true for you as well. This is where it is vital to appreciate and celebrate aspects of yourself based on who God says you are through time reading His Word. What does the Bible say of you as a creation of God? He says you are unique (Psalm 139:13), special (Ephesians 2:10), lovely (Daniel 12:3), precious (1 Corinthians 6:20), chosen (John 15:16), and loved (John 3:16). If you are doing better than you were a year ago, well done. If you are doing poorly compared to how you were a year ago, what do you need to help you along the way? Is it rest? Is it a kind ear to listen? Is it therapy or rehabilitation for part of your heart and mind? It's true that you and I are "not enough"—we need something we don't have to help us reach our full potential. We need Jesus as our role model to help us through every situation we encounter in life.

There is also the aspect of the power of words. If someone makes a grating remark about you, you have the choice to allow what is said to hold weight in your life or not. You can choose to let it penetrate your soul, your identity, and your self-perception, or to let it roll off you like water off a duck's back. The same is true if you speak it over yourself. You have the choice to speak kindly to yourself or to be your own bully. Make the choice to speak well over the vessel of the Spirit of God you are. As my pastor once said while placing his hand over his heart, "This is God's house; how will I treat (or speak over) God's house?"

One of the greatest areas where people can feel they are not enough is their femininity or masculinity. Assumptions are quickly made about even young children as they are forming their self-perceptions. Telling a young person that they are not enough in an area, especially connected to being feminine or masculine enough, can be excessively damaging to an impressionable child who is still figuring out if they prefer the color blue or green, let alone anything else. It also creates a great divide, an "us vs. them" mentality that is pernicious to the child in their upbringing to believe that such a practice is acceptable. It is not. Men and women are more than stereotypes.

One of my friends has a toddler son who had asked for a baby doll to play with. Her sisters condemned her for buying the doll, for they believe baby dolls to be a toy reserved only for little girls. What hogwash. Thankfully my friend knew that her son could have a baby doll and still be fully and completely the masculine boy he is inside and out. It did not cancel out how he was designed to be, and in fact it will help make him a better husband and father one day. Society can be so naive as to think that cultivating qualities such as compassion, consideration, and softness in caring for a baby doll somehow nullifies a child to be "a man." This young boy is so gentle and sweet with the doll, and as he grows or perhaps one day receives a little sibling, he will know how to care for others. The doll did not thwart his masculine energy, but it taught him what it means to be a man—a protector with a tender heart and a peaceful nature.

In addition, in our society a man is often looked upon as not being masculine if he cries, or as acting more like a woman if he feels very deeply about something. In Scripture, David was a fierce warrior who as a teen defeated not only Goliath, but literal bears and lions. He led armies and an entire kingdom, but he wasn't just this muscular leader. That was not the only side of David. David was a musician, poet, artist, and an incredibly deep feeler. Most of the psalms were written by David and express vast feelings of joy, sorrow, love, and desire. These psalms reveal he was not afraid to cry, to weep, to embrace all that he was made to be by God as an artist, a dreamer, and fully as a man. We must not be so narrow-minded to think that emotion is reserved for only one gender.

On the other side there is pressure on young girls to dress and act in a certain way to be considered feminine. One of the greatest movies that absolutely voids that idea is *A League of Their Own* starring Geena Davis and Tom Hanks. The film takes place during World War II while all able-bodied men were sent off to war. The country is in desperate need of morale, so one of the sponsors of the men's baseball team takes the initiative to put together a league of all women baseball players. These women can throw fastballs, hit home runs, and play just as hard as any man, all while wearing a dress. The film showcases that women can be feminine, while at the same time enjoying and partaking in a game previously reserved for men. Standing confident in who you are regardless of the evaluations of others, entwined with the joy that comes from simply being you, is infectiously wonderful. A little girl can be both feminine in her own way and a full-on tomboy getting mud-smeared playing with the boys. She does not lose her femininity, but she embraces all that makes her, her.

We could also consider Jael in the book of Judges. Women are not often thought of as warriors, and especially in biblical times there was a clear delineation in who did the physical fighting, but Jael is a prime example of a fierce woman. It had been prophesied by Deborah that the human hand that would be used to defeat the evil Sisera would be that of a woman (Judges 4:9). This broke the assumption that only men would be used by God in such a way. Jael's bravery in defeating Sisera did not take away from her femininity or her womanhood; rather, it showed that we are multifaceted humans capable of being used by God in limitless ways.

Reassessing our ideas of what is enough and what is not enough is long overdue. Instead of casting judgment over yourself and others, know that humans are incredibly dynamic creatures capable of myriad emotions, interests, and abilities. We are not as black and white as common stereotypes make us out to be, and there is nothing wrong with existing in the gray overlap of things. It is proof that God designed each of us as multifarious personalities. Allow your brain to comprehend that you can be of such caliber and conclude that you are only in competition with the you of yesterday. Remember the wise words of Eleanor Roosevelt, "Nobody can make you feel inferior without your consent." Say that out loud: no one can make you feel inferior without your consent.

TOO MUCH

There also exists the sentiment among us Wallflowers that while we may feel we are not enough in some areas, we are *too much* in others. Too loud, too quiet, too silly, too serious; the list goes on and on. These are not always labels we put on ourselves but ones that are given to us by others. But is it that you're really *too much*, or is it that you're just around people who aren't used to your way of doing things?

To some, the feeling of rejection can seem like a bitter jab, pernicious in effect. Not just the feeling of rejection for being picked last for a sports team, but the kind of rejection that really hits, that leaves you questioning your own worth and value. The kind that alludes that what you bring to the table is not just an alternative taste, but that the whole of you is shot down and unwanted all in one fail swoop. In some cases, you may even feel that if someone cannot accept you for who you really are, who ever could? Can you even ever accept you, or should you join with them in rejecting who you are as to somehow shield and protect your heart from ever feeling such a sting again? Rejection feels like being so distasteful you're vomited up and left for dead.

Being told you are too much coupled with a fear of further rejection invokes a sort of self-sabotage. Self-sabotaging comes into play when the desire to be all you could be, to be authentic and genuine to who you really are, is hijacked by fear. This fear stifles your actions, leading you to not even try—because if you don't try, you can't fail, right? But that fear also kills the ability for you to be able to reach the true potential of all you could be, all you could create, and all you could bring of light, love, and invention to the world. You behave in a way to keep those around you more comfortable, as you make an effort to become smaller and more digestible in fear of being too much. Self-sabotage in a sense kills your potential.

So, what are specific ways to fix fear ruling your life? First, there is the conscious decision to stop giving self-sabotage a weapon to cut off your potential. That could very well look like shutting your mouth, taking a breath before an action, or pushing yourself to take a step out on the ledge in courage. If you have found in the past that you sabotage relationships by speaking in such a way that it harms the core integrity of the relationship, make a mindful decision to think before you speak. If you have already said something crippling to the relationship, see how you can make amends to perhaps restore the connection. If it is truly beyond repair, there is then the lesson you take with you in the future to not repeat the same mistake. Learn from the mistake, but don't wear the mistake as identity. Glean from the wisdom that is apparent to you now in the consequence of the mistake, but don't allow it to happen again within your power.

In the same vein, try to consider the consequences of an action before taking it. In essence, read the room.

Know when it is appropriate to make a move and when it is best to redirect, shift your approach, or save the action for a time when it will be better received. This doesn't mean you are stifling yourself, but it means that you are using context clues to bring forward what you desire to share in the right timing and place. Sometimes it is best to save the dessert for last instead of offering a full Baked Alaska at six in the morning.

My dear friend Sara once found a beautiful charcoal drawing in a thrift store that just captivated her. Someone had donated it and the thrift store placed its value at thirteen dollars. Sara knew there was something unique about this piece and she had it appraised. As it turned out, the drawing was an original Cameron Booth drawing with an auction value of around three hundred to six hundred dollars. What one person saw as worthless enough to give to a thrift store, and what a thrift store saw as having a value of only thirteen dollars, art professionals saw as having a value of hundreds of dollars. So, perhaps you're in the wrong place and that is why your value isn't being recognized. More than anything you must realize that your true inherent worth is not rooted in man, but in God. Psalm 139 reminds us that God crafted each one of us and He knew us before the beginning of time. Your worth is not dependent on the opinions of others or the assumptions of those around you; rather, it is rooted in the fact that the Creator of the universe loves you so much that He gave His only Son to die for you so you could have a personal relationship with Him.

Finally, there are times when you must push yourself to get back out there. You may not feel ready, you may lack the boldness you feel necessary to do it, but you will never know if you don't try. If you flop, then consider where it flopped and what to do differently; but, to your surprise, you might just find yourself flying. A bird never soared sitting still.

It is important to realize that what some consider *too much*, others will find satisfactory or perhaps the most glorious portion there ever could be. The stomach of one is not the stomach of another, and you might be presenting yourself to the wrong person. Think of it in the way of meals you can purchase at a restaurant. Some have the capacity to handle only a side order of fries; a full meal would send them over the top. For others, a super-sized meal is the bare minimum of what their stomachs require for sustenance. Perhaps you are presenting yourself to someone who can consume only that side order of fries, and you are a wonderfully crafted super-size of a meal. Graciously forgive the person for their poor reactions, rejections, or mishandling of your heart and then acknowledge that they are not the one to receive the fullness of you. Then consider the hopeful truth that there is the great potential that one day you will find that person who has been longing for, hoping for, and aching for that full extra value meal. You are not "too much"; you are just enough for the right person.

Don't lessen yourself, diminish yourself, or demean yourself to make others find you more acceptable. You cheat the world of all that you could possibly be in this world by trying to make the small environment of those around you feel less awkward. Think of how many musicians and artists held back all they could be to keep the status quo with those around them. Do you really want to waste all that could possibly be to not cause a ripple in the water? Honey, cause a hurricane with this one life God has given you.

THE BEAUTIFUL LETDOWN

Have you ever had someone say to you, or have you ever said to yourself, "Why can't you be like everyone else?" Wallflowers can especially have this nagging belief that they would be far happier or better off if they were no longer themselves, but instead were cookie cutter, normal, and a perfect fit for the masses. Have you ever considered that it's a gift to be different? Have you considered that there is something beautiful about being what some might even consider "a letdown"?

So often we find ourselves desperately trying to fit into the world, but the truth of the matter is that we do not belong here. As those who have placed our faith in Christ, all of eternity awaits us in our true home of heaven. It is when we stop trying to win the approval of man that we can experience the freedom, the joy, and the opportunity to live out the life God has for us to live in and through Him.

During Christ's ministry on earth, He did not come only for those who knew God already, and He did not limit His ministry to those whom many assumed He would minister to. As we explored earlier in Matthew 9, Christ sat with those no one wanted anything to do with. I love the lyrics of "A Beautiful Letdown" by Switchfoot:

> We are a beautiful letdown, painfully uncool
> The church of the dropouts, the losers, the sinners,
> the failures and the fools[3]

It's the different individuals who add color to this world. They add spice to the melting pot of us all and bring about the shift from mundane to marvelous. Van Gogh said, "Normality is a paved road: It's comfortable to walk, but no flowers grow on it." Those who are different are the flowers that grow, and don't you want to be a wildflower of the field?

Madam C. J. Walker was someone who lived this out well. She was the first self-made female millionaire in America, and it all was spurred not by luck but by stepping out of the norm and being different, true to what she knew she was capable of and more. Madam C. J. Walker was born Sarah Breedlove in 1867 to former slaves turned sharecroppers. She married very young, at the age of fourteen, and was left a widow at age twenty with a young daughter to care for. To make matters in her life worse she found herself suffering from hair loss, more than likely caused by stress and other natural factors. In an age where the normal solution would be to comply with her fate in poverty, Sarah stepped out to be different. She took the initiative to work as a laundress and cook, and later became a saleswoman for hair care products she had begun using. Shortly after moving to Denver, she developed her own product line and went into business for herself. She made the courageous choice to be different with no indication that it would yield any result. She found massive success in her endeavors and established a system to help black women become financially secure in their own right, at a time when that concept was nearly impossible. WomensHistory.org shares,

An advocate of black women's economic independence, she opened training programs in the "Walker System" for her national network of licensed sales agents who earned healthy commissions. Ultimately, Walker employed 40,000 African American women and men in the US, Central America, and the Caribbean. She also founded the National Negro Cosmetics Manufacturers Association in 1917.

Walker's business grew rapidly, with sales exceeding $500,000 in the final year of her life. Her total worth topped $1 million, and included a mansion in Irvington, New York, dubbed "Villa Lewaro," and properties in Harlem, Chicago, Pittsburgh, and St. Louis.

As her wealth increased, so did her philanthropic and political outreach. Walker contributed to the YMCA, covered tuition for six African American students at Tuskegee Institute, and became active in the anti-lynching movement, donating $5,000 to the NAACP's efforts. Just prior to dying of kidney failure, Walker revised her will, bequeathing two-thirds of future net profits to charity, as well as thousands of dollars to various individuals and schools.[4]

Madam C. J. Walker broke from the status quo, refusing to stay at home or work simple jobs as most women in her time did. And because she made such a shift, she not only changed the lives of countless people, she also changed the world.

Another story of a unique individual who became a difference maker was Charlie Chaplin. Charlie Chaplin was born in 1889 in London, the son of entertainers. Chaplin from a very young age presented the ability to make others laugh; from slapstick action to his wit, there was something about him that mustered up contagious laughter. In 1913, after a few years on stage as a comedian, he was invited to come to America to take a swing behind the camera. Film was still a very new and experimental medium, one that in its early age kept a very uniform and strict set of rules. Chaplin found nearly overnight success with American audiences with the introduction of his original character "the Tramp." This character did not look like the usual clown or jester. From his waddling gate to his iconic outfit, the Tramp was certainly unique. What Chaplin introduced to comedy was something delightful, something that was different and new but that would shape how comedy would be presented for years to come. Even with the introduction of "talkies" or speaking films, Chaplin held a vital role in the progress of filmmaking. His film *Modern Times* merged the classic silent-film comedy with audible dialogue. The film inspired genera-tions to come, and all because one man tried a different concept of what comedy could be, whether presented in front of a single viewer or a massive audience.

We would be lacking to not include someone who co-founded a company whose slogan for several years was "Think Different": Steve Jobs of Apple. Steve Jobs broke with the flow early in life. A college dropout, he stepped out of the idea that success would come only from a col-lege degree and with great enthusiasm pursued the idea of doing things in a different manner. When his friend Steve Wozniak designed a unique concept of computer, Jobs knew that the new Apple I could be used as a per-sonal tool, not just for business. He pitched the product to investors and acquired what was needed to get Apple off the ground. The vision and ambition to do things differently never left Jobs, and beyond Apple he was an intrinsic part of Pixar in its early days. He was a major contributor to *Toy Story*, the first computer-animated feature film. Unconventional and avant-garde Jobs made "thinking different" a way of life.

Being unlike everyone else does not guarantee that you'll find success in the way of fame or money, but you will change the world. You can offer the world something that only you can give, something that the world would lack without your thumbprint upon it. Take off the gloves you wear to keep that thumbprint from being stamped, because you might just start something remarkable. Remarkable in the way that your thumbprint will be re-marked, marked again and again for years to come in a world that needs it desperately.

Are you who you want to be? Are you perhaps even limiting all you could be? God can do more in your life than all you could ask for, hope for, dream for, or imagine, so what if you are limiting God by just what you can imagine? What if?

PERSONAL REFLECTION
AND APPLICATION QUESTIONS

1. Have you identified a soul-wound that has shifted your approach toward life? What does God say about that wound? Will you make the choice to seek His help for forgiveness and healing?

2. Where do you need a new scale or measuring stick for being enough?

3. In what area do you need to stop self-sabotaging and make a dramatic move forward?

4. What would breaking from the crowd in a small way look like for you today?

CHAPTER 3

Digging In

To live is the rarest thing in the world.
Most people exist, that is all.

—Oscar Wilde

I came that they may have life,
and have it abundantly.

—Jesus (John 10:10, NASB95)

THE BULLY IN THE MIRROR

If I were to ask you to visualize a bully, the first image to enter your mind would probably be a cartoon bully, a movie character like Biff in *Back to the Future,* or someone from your past. More than likely that person somehow had the innate ability to find that one specific string to pluck that could instantly demoralize you, making you feel as if you were worthless and meaningless. Yet what we seldom realize is that there is a bully far closer than you think, and you see that person every morning in the mirror when you wake up. For many of us Wallflowers, the most significant bully we encounter is ourselves through how we speak to or treat ourselves.

The concept you hold of yourself will be evident to others in subtle ways. As much as we think self-esteem and self-concept are aspects we can hide within the lockets of our hearts, we aren't really fooling anyone. The way you carry yourself—from your stride to your demeanor—reveals how you view yourself. That is not said to somehow hold the perceptions of others at a higher esteem than they ought to be, but you are setting an example that other people may emulate. Others, especially impressionable youth, will see how you carry yourself, how you treat yourself, and your self-perception, and may adopt aspects of what they see in their own behavior. How we treat ourselves has more of an impact than we know on those around us. How then can we heal from this and stop bullying ourselves?

It begins with the ongoing narrative you have in your own head. Let's start at a very basic level. What do you call yourself? What name do you use when giving yourself a pep talk or a lashing? I call myself "Cal," not "Cally." For me it is not a nickname, but a term of familiarity that is reserved for behind closed doors. In fact, though I never correct anyone, there are very, very few select persons I am genuinely comfortable with calling me "Cal." Those who I am not comfortable with using my nickname are on my unofficial "do not 'Cal' list."

What name do you have for yourself that a very select few if any may call you? Why did you choose that name (if you did), and what connotations does that name carry? Is it a name that you have a healthy respect for, and if the answer to that is "no," how can you heal that? Perhaps it is best to choose a new self-name, as what we call ourselves entwines with our very identity. Calling yourself names such as "idiot" or "stupid" is demeaning at the innermost level. That's not your real name, so stop calling yourself by counterfeit names. You know how Starbucks almost always will get your name wrong, or spell it wrong, and you brush it off, but sometimes there is that annoying itchy feeling because they don't really know you? Or that one person who never gets your name right and makes you feel so unknown? You place that same feeling upon yourself when you use a self-deprecating word regarding who you are. That is not your name, so stop answering to it. That welcomes our next matter of the inner narrative moving forward.

How do you speak to yourself? Are you quick to make a snide remark such as, "You idiot, you can't do anything right," or are you more forgiving? Do you beat yourself up in that narrative in a way that you would never dream of speaking to another human being with such rude insults? Studies have shown that if we speak to plants with kindness, they thrive; do you consider yourself less than a plant? This isn't just how we treat others; it's how we treat ourselves. If you cannot speak kindly and honor yourself, how then can you expect anyone else to? If you want to be someone who speaks with words laced in grace and honey, it begins with how you speak to the inner you.

Healing the inner narrative is vital to a healthier self-concept and rehabilitating the bully within toward a better path. You will have to work to take captive your every thought, every sneer, and every quick-witted jeering punch within. We must also realize that we have an Enemy who is the father of lies, and he loves to mimic your voice, pose as you, and speak lies. This is why we must take every thought captive, as Paul encourages in 2 Corinthians 10:5: "We demolish arguments and every pretension that sets itself up against the knowledge of God, and we take captive every thought to make it obedient to Christ." God does not call you words such as "stupid" or "ugly," so when you hear such a thought in your head, identify it as a lie, capture it, and submit it to Christ. It's not a one and done; you need to be diligent. But the more you train yourself to speak in kindness and offer grace to yourself, the more you will be able to do the same with those around you. The more you reframe your mistakes as learning lessons and hold them to a high expectation of a learning tool, not an enabling tactic or a failure flag, you will be able to teach that to others. The adolescents around you will develop a more life-giving approach when they see you making strides in your own path. Even friends around you will reconsider how they operate within, and who knows what kind of good trend you could begin?

Recognizing that the bully within you could be a large shadow with the inner root of fear—fear of all that you lack, all that you fail at, and all that you fear in rebuke from others—shifts your view of the bully. That bully is not really the genuine "you" but rather can be a Frankenstein-like collection of every opinion, judgment, or prejudice you have received or have witnessed. Whether the bully originates within you or is the voice of the Enemy, when such negativity emerges you must not allow it to hold a position of value in your life. You hold the power to either let that bully remain a loud, obnoxious voice or shut it down. This doesn't mean you will suddenly interact in the world perfectly, and it does not mean others won't continue to act as they always have, but what it does mean is that you no longer reject yourself for what you do or what you might potentially do. It means you extend the same kindness, grace, and encouragement within that you offer to others. The bully in the mirror does not have to remain there, and aren't some of our favorite stories the ones in which the villains turn from their ways to live in peace and harmony with others? Let's see that story written and lived out in your life through loving the "you" part of that bully until she becomes a friend.

FEELING IT

I have this really strong desire to one day go to a restaurant with a reservation made under the name "Pity" just so they'll call out over the loudspeaker, "Pity, Party of one, your table is ready." Perhaps you will disagree, but in my own humble opinion we are all justified in having a pity party of one on occasion. Not a long, drawn-out party, but one where that need to sit and stew for a bit is satisfied.

Consider it in this way. If you sit in the dirt a few hours, just long enough to stew and leave an imprint of your caboose in the dirt and then you get up and move forward, you can look back and see you had your time to sit and stew. The imprint in the dirt is evidence enough that you had your sectioned-off allotment and you got it out of your system. You can then move on knowing you let yourself feel it for a bit.

Really feeling something—be it pain, be it sadness, be it anything—is proof that you are alive and not merely existing. How many of us function in such an apathetic numbness that we are eating, drinking, sleeping, and operating in daily tasks but inside we are about as alive as a robot? That's no way to live; in fact, it is not living whatsoever. For a very long time in my own life, I would say—whether in my own head, to a friend, or even in prayer—that I just wanted to die. I think God allowed me to feel it for long enough before He hit me with a truth so hard it made me shift my repetitive complaint. He explained to me it wasn't that I wanted to die, rather I wanted to not just merely exist. He knew I wanted to live, and actually live. That set me on a quest of what it really means to live, and I dare say it, live abundantly. That truth was a great gift to me, but I am so very grateful I had my time to be a ratty little grump about things when I needed it.

If you do not allow yourself to have it and to get it out, then it will manifest itself in other ways. This is why vices like drinking, smoking, gambling, or binging become habits. We are releasing it in some way, healthy or not. This is not to say that there are not healthy ways to let out frustration, aggression, or disappointments, because that is possible too. If you have never tried it, a batting cage is a wondrous place to let out energy, as is chopping wood, using a punching bag, or writing a seething letter that you'll never send. Those don't hurt other people or you (be careful on the axe thing, though) and they bring about catharsis. One of my youth kids was going through a hard time with a toxic coworker, and my first protective thought wanted to say, "If you wanna burn a bridge, I got a match." But after checking myself I instead said, "Would it help to go throw ice cubes at trees?" It was a pop-fly ball coming from left field, but she was in, and it offered her a tangible way to release her anger with no harm to the environment or to anyone else. The key is you don't stay in that mindset for too long. It's not a place to lay your hat, it's a place to get it out.

Validating yourself is also a way to give yourself grace. You are valid to feel and to express your feelings, from grief or to relief. Humans are gloriously dynamic in that we can in one instant experience a plethora of emotions. You are not limited or so one-dimensional that you can feel only one thing at a time. Processing what you are feeling in the swirl of chaos can also help you sort through what is needed for your life to go on in the future. If you bottled up the chaos it will not ferment into something tasteful, but if you take the time to do the work as it is happening or shortly afterward, you will not turn bitter yourself. Consider how even David went through seasons of depression. He allowed himself to feel the ache, to express the pain through writing and prayer, and he did not stifle or hide his raw emotion. Psalm 13 offers great imagery of this:

> How long, LORD? Will you forget me forever?
>> How long will you hide your face from me?
> How long must I wrestle with my thoughts
>> and day after day have sorrow in my heart?
>> How long will my enemy triumph over me?
>
> Look on me and answer, LORD my God.
>> Give light to my eyes, or I will sleep in death,
> and my enemy will say, "I have overcome him,"
>> and my foes will rejoice when I fall.
>
> But I trust in your unfailing love;
>> my heart rejoices in your salvation.
> I will sing the LORD's praise,
>> for he has been good to me. (Psalm 13:1–6)

What is clear in this passage is that David permitted himself to be honest with himself and with God about how he felt. He did not condemn himself for the emotions, but he did not stay in a place of self-pity either. We can learn much from David in the catharsis of writing and prayer. He did not allow such real feelings to define the situation, and he reminded his heart that God is bigger than his current circumstances and problems. Be like David—feel it, don't just ignore it.

DEPRESSION

Perhaps the best metaphor to describe depression is that of the weather. You are out enjoying a sunny day, when suddenly dark and heavy clouds begin to form. You give them no mind, for they are not anything too concerning, and perhaps may fade away quickly. When they do not, and those clouds begin to darken even more, it becomes concerning. The thunder begins, as does the lightning, and suddenly you are soaking wet in the middle of the storm, unable to find a way out. The storm rages, surrounding you in a plethora of doubt, insecurities, false perceptions, and confusion. You do not know if it is light peeking through the clouds, or another lightning bolt striking. Your tears only seem to mesh with the copious downpours, and you for a time forget what it was like to live in the sunny day. Unsure of how long this storm will last, you sit and look for a way out, but you find nothing. This is what depression feels like.

I heard a friend once refer to himself as "the king of depression," and he shared how he stopped resisting and allowed God to pull him out. That makes me think of the story of Martin Luther, who was caught in a wretched lightning storm in the early 1500s and called out to God. It radically changed Luther to the point that he put aside his career as a lawyer and devoted his entire life to ministry. What a way for God to pull someone out of a storm, eh?

What is important to acknowledge about depression and anxiety is that they are real, and that they are present. Pretending that they are not is like pretending that it is not raining when you are soaking wet in the middle of a storm. There is no "key" to escaping that storm. Antidepressants can act as incredible umbrellas at times, but they do not stop the storm. They can lessen the impact, but the storm is still raging about. God is the only One who can cease the storm.

In Luke 8, we see the account of Jesus quieting the storm by merely speaking to it:

> One day Jesus said to his disciples, "Let's cross to the other side of the lake." So they got into a boat and started out. As they sailed across, Jesus settled down for a nap. But soon a fierce storm came down on the lake. The boat was filling with water, and they were in real danger.
>
> The disciples went and woke him up, shouting, "Master, Master, we're going to drown!"
>
> When Jesus woke up, he rebuked the wind and the raging waves. Suddenly the storm stopped and all was calm. Then he asked them, "Where is your faith?"
>
> The disciples were terrified and amazed. "Who is this man?" they asked each other. "When he gives a command, even the wind and waves obey him!" (Luke 8:22–26, NLT)

What if Jesus does not stop the storm? This is something in my own life I've often found relevant, and it is a reminder of Paul's thorn. Paul speaks of a thorn in his side in 2 Corinthians 12. He never specifically shares what the thorn was, just that it was there and that God would not remove it no matter how many times Paul begged. Depression and anxiety can often be an enduring thorn of sorts. It is vital to recognize that we cannot tell depression to merely go away and have it obey. We cannot decide to just be happy and see the storm dissipate. We cannot control the storm, but we can press into the One who can. We can realize that in our weakness, He is stronger. That is where the real shift in the atmosphere can occur.

In our weakness, He is strong. In His strength then, we can be fragile and weak and can rest. Matthew 11:28–30 promises, "Come to me, all you who are weary and burdened, and I will give you rest. Take my yoke upon you and learn from me, for I am gentle and humble in heart, and you will find rest for your souls. For my yoke is easy and my burden is light." Jesus wants to take our depression from us. He wants the struggle, the tears, the blood-curdling screams our souls cry out when we try to vocalize the lie that we are fine. He wants to take that upon Himself, and in return give us rest. He wants to give us love. He wants to give us peace. He wants to give us Himself.

To paint it another way, consider the 2000 movie *Cast Away* with Tom Hanks. In the film the main character,

Chuck Noland, finds himself stranded on a remote island all alone. This film is not one where he finds rest or beauty on a deserted island, rather the dampening reality of what it looks like to be trapped, unsure if life could ever change. The audience is given a glimpse over the course of four years of how he meets his basic needs to survive while also making every attempt to escape. Not to spoil the film, but against all odds one fateful day in the form of an unlikely asset a sail washes upon the shore, allowing Noland to prevail over the waves that were previously insurmountable. Toward the end of the film he sits with his friend summing up all that he had experienced:

> I was never gonna get off that island. I was gonna die there, totally alone. I was gonna get sick, or get injured or something. The only choice I had, the only thing I could control was when, and how, and where it was going to happen. So...I made a rope and I went up to the summit, to hang myself. I had to test it, you know? Of course. You know me. And the weight of the log, snapped the limb of the tree, so I-I - , I couldn't even kill myself the way I wanted to. I had power over *nothing*. And that's when this feeling came over me like a warm blanket. I knew, somehow, that I had to stay alive. Somehow. I had to keep breathing. Even though there was no reason to hope. And all my logic said that I would never see this place again. So that's what I did. I stayed alive. I kept breathing. And one day my logic was proven all wrong because the tide came in and gave me a sail.

And now, here I am. I'm back. In Memphis, talking to you. I have ice in my glass. And I know what I have to do now. I gotta keep breathing. Because tomorrow the sun will rise. Who knows what the tide could bring?[5]

Against all logic, against all that tangibly could be considered, help arrived. The beauty of this film is that it symbolizes so much without over-explaining anything. The "warm" feeling Noland is referencing was God, and a beyond-logic push to keep living, to keep walking, to keep surviving. Sure enough, in time a sail arrived, and with it the freedom Noland was waiting for so desperately.

I have a great fondness for this film not only for the message it conveys, or the hope it offers, but for the push it gave me in a very dark time. When I was twenty-six, a horrific and traumatizing event occurred in my life, one so debilitating my brain blacked out the memory. The memory was triggered years later and with it I found myself very shattered within. No matter how hard I tried to move on with my life, I kept feeling thrust back into the jarring event; in truth it felt like a prison. The pernicious voice of the suicide demon whispered defeating ideas into my mind, and I grew weary. I knew that was not the voice of God, and I knew that was not my voice, but it felt inexhaustible. Oddly enough God kept nudging me to go to a second-hand book and movie store, so I complied. There, prominently displayed on the end cap, almost like it was waiting for me, was the movie *Cast Away*. I had seen the film several times through the years, but the DVD seemed to beckon me to bring it home. That DVD held within it a story of a man, barely surviving like myself, and in the end a message of hope: "Who knows what the tide could bring?" As much as I questioned why God had allowed that event to happen to me, as much as I wrestled within about why traumatic things happen and evil reigns in this world, it seemed God had answered me with the parable of Chuck Noland.

The event did happen, but God in His goodness allowed for a peace to warmly wash over me that this wasn't the end of my story. In time a sail came, and I did escape that metaphoric island. The beauty of God is that He does not always answer in the way we want, rather, in the way we need. Even after the storm was over, it took time for me to move forward. As Haruki Murakami said, "And once the storm is over, you won't remember how you made it through, how you managed to survive. You won't even be sure, whether the storm is really over. But one thing is certain. When you come out of the storm, you won't be the same person who walked in. That's what this storm's all about."

Parables in movies, a verse, a word, encouragement through a friend, or just the feeling of a peace that goes beyond logic or understanding are ways He might use to bring you out of your own time of feeling there is no escape. What is vital is that we hold firm to the knowledge that He is still working, so don't give up before the story is over. Don't give up; your story isn't over.

PERSONAL REFLECTION
AND APPLICATION QUESTIONS

1. What do you call yourself? Do you call yourself "idiot" or "dummy" or "stupid"? How can you shift those names to be ones that are endearing and kind?

2. What is a healthy way for you to "feel it" and cathartically release?

3. If you personally have battled suicidal thoughts, or someone you love has, how can you offer more grace and love toward that soul?

CHAPTER 4

Pruning

Holy Spirit make me more like Jesus,
every day a little more like Jesus.
Crucify my flesh with Yours
that my new life might be secured.
Everything I do, done so I can honor You.
Resurrect me, sanctify me, make me into Your image.
—**Canaan Baca, "More Like Jesus"**

Don't doubt your value. Don't run from who you are.
—**Aslan**

HEALING WEAPONIZED WORDS

Sticks and stones aside, words hold greater power than we may realize. Words can have a potent effect, and can slash or encourage a soul. This is true not only in how we speak to others but in how we speak to ourselves as well. Language has the inherent ability to be meaningful and lovely, to invoke deep emotions that yield confidence and joy, but also to wound someone's innermost being regarding their self-concept or self-worth. It has the ability for a play on words or for a single word to have multiple meanings depending upon tone, a person's mental connection to the word, and other factors. These words hold powerful gunpowder within them, and recall that gun powder can shoot deadly bullets or burst beautiful fireworks in the sky depending on the circumstance. That is why we must consider how the words said about and to you, be it by someone else or yourself, make an impact completely contingent upon your line of thought. Their meaning can shift depending on your interpretation.

For example, consider the word "nerd." Nerd is commonly associated with someone who is not considered popular, charismatic, or cool due to their substantial knowledge in a particular field. Nerds stand out because they know more than the rest, which intimidates those around them, or their hyperfocus on an area of study brings them ridicule for being different. But what if we reframed our connotations with that word? What if instead of looking at it as a negative to be full of knowledge with a subject, we instead considered "nerd" a compliment? For what a wonderful attribute it really is to have substantial knowledge surrounding a subject or area of study. Is it really that bad to have a passion and aptitude for learning in a particular field of study? How does that make you less of a person or not compelling and interesting? Isn't it instead something wonderfully unique about you? Something others might aspire to be like? What a marvelous thing it is to be so immersed in a subject that you are considered a "nerd" for it!

Take all the associations you have concerning a word and dissect the word into its pessimistic and optimistic meanings, and then reframe your definition so that the word is no longer a weapon to harm you personally. Weaponized words flipped on end can turn from that which was used to attack you into a great asset for you. For what you once saw in a negative way is instead seen as something you are confident of yourself in; it is self-affirming. In essence you are saying, "Why, yes! I am very capable, I have such a wealth of knowledge, and I appreciate that others see that as well. What a gift it is that I have been given a brain that can contain such a wealth of knowledge and that I can use it in application, and I find joy in exploring subjects." The word that was once meant for your harm is now something that you wear with a smile when it is said of you. By changing your frame of mind, it can become part of your own arsenal.

Another word we could consider is "weird," such as, "She's so weird." Why is weird a bad thing? What if being weird is actually a treasured gift? You don't fit into the mainstream, but why should you? You're not one of the crowd, you're one of a kind. You are quirky, a bit odd, not everyone's taste, but to the right ones you are a wonderful and rare gem. The kind of gem that someone will go to great lengths to protect, honor, and hold dear. Many of the things one would consider weird someone else thinks the sun rises and sets with. I heard it said once, "You've got to be odd to be number one"; it's a good math pun and it's true. The greatest artists of all time have been straight up weirdos, but weirdos add color to the world. Francis Bacon once noted, "There is no exquisite beauty without some strangeness in the proportion." Amen to that. So, shine out vibrantly in your own kind of weird, because the world could use a cup of radiance only the weird ones can bring. One thing is for sure about those who are "weird"—they are unforgettable and irreplaceable. You aren't replaceable, remember that.

One more with a little story about the genesis of this practice.

When I was in third-grade math, we were learning what a remainder was. For those who have been out of school for some time and need a refresher, a remainder is what is left over after doing a division problem. For example, in five divided by two, you have two groups of two and a remainder of one. One is the loneliest number, isn't it? It sure felt that way in the third grade, to the point that my eight-year-old self concluded that she was the remainder at school. Honestly, I wasn't wrong; I *was* the loner. Being a loner or the remainder was something I considered bad for so many years, but over time I realized what a gift it is to be the remainder, the loner. It is a gift in the way that it has given me the freedom to be fully and authentically myself. It is not some curse, and it does not mean that I don't have any friends or close companions; rather, I no longer feel the need to be part of a group in order to have an identity or find worth.

My identity and worth are not contingent upon other people. My identity is independent of the opinion of other human beings, and it is rooted in Someone far bigger than myself. It is held securely in Someone I will never lose, and who knows me in the most pure, raw, and the most intricate of ways, for my worth is found in Christ. If it were not for the gift of being a loner and remainder, I may not have realized what a gift it is that everything about me is not dependent upon something or someone I might lose.

As Einstein wisely put it, "Be a loner. That gives you time to wonder, to search for the truth. Have holy curiosity. Make your life worth living." Or to put it in other terms, being a loner allows me to be within and without. One of the most radiate scenes in *The Great Gatsby* is when Nick, the narrator, offers, "I was within and without, simultaneously enchanted and repelled by the inexhaustible variety of life." Loners secure the authority in their own lives as to how much they are within or without an occasion, and what a gift that really can be.

This practice of reframing hurtful terms can be applied to a multitude of words. It does not eliminate the feeling that certain words have been used to hurt you, and if you do not think redefining those words can lessen their sting, then try to disregard them. It is okay to take your time in this practice, or to accept that some words are not meant to be reframed. Remember, you hold the eraser for those words, and you can choose to wear them or to ignore them. They only hold the power you give them. One person's poor use of language and ability to speak is not your portion to accept in this world. You are not the sum of the opinions of others; in fact, the opinions of others can shift as quickly as the clouds in the sky. Your feelings about the words are valid, but you are also completely in control of how you let words affect your self-perception. We can allow the words spoken about and to us to be inserted within the bags we carry with us, or to be thrown into the gutter never to be brought up again. This is where our own language and the ability to utter "no" is so vitally important. Let your communication be rooted in honesty and belief.

Ask yourself what words you can collect in your own arsenal to use not only in defense of yourself but in defining yourself in a positive and healthy way. How would you define your work ethic? How would you define your best qualities, and how can you reframe the ones that are not as adorned in lace to be ones that are works in progress? What areas of life are you seeking to improve on, and how can you use the power of language to help you be more kind to others and yourself? How can you use words to leave a mark and not a stain?

A mark was left on my heart one winter evening several years ago completely reframing the word "quiet." I was out with a few friends and my friend brought her new boyfriend. By nature I am quite shy and quiet, but to please people and adapt to my surroundings, I've developed the habit of forcing myself to talk even when I have nothing significant to say. This night I was feeling worn from the workweek and I simply did not have the energy to play the outgoing friend. I spoke as I felt led, but I did not push myself to fill gaps in the conversation with chatter and instead offered a friendly smile. Her boyfriend made a few comments about how quiet I was, not in an endearing or complementary tone but in a way that felt unaccepting.

On the drive home that night, I beat myself up relentlessly in my mind asking myself, *Why can't you be different? Why can't you just talk and be more normal?* I was gently interrupted by God as He whispered, "You don't need to change yourself to make others like you." He told me that I was created to be quiet, for when I speak my words are impactful and to be heard. My complaints fell silent, and my tears streamed down my face as I felt so accepted, cherished, and embraced for who I really am. God spoke to me in that whisper, and I was able to see that "quiet" is no longer a stain of a word, but a beautifully gentle mark of the Creator's thumbprint on me in the way I was crafted. What words need to be a mark and not a stain in your own life?

DEAR YOUNG ME

In college, my preferred therapeutic release for just about any emotion was songwriting. Writing has always been an area where I feel uninhibited and permitted to pour out all that is trapped within me. After running into an ex-boyfriend at an open mic coffee house, I wrote a song entitled "Leather Shoes" that includes this lyric: "You fit like my old leather shoes. But then I remember and the sole falls through. You think by now of the lessons that I've learned, I'd realize the past is a place you can't return." These were the words of an emotional twenty-two-year-old, and while the past is indeed a lovely place we like to visit, we can't return there. In fact, just like old, worn-out shoes, perhaps we should consider letting it go in many ways.

Memory lane can be a block of beautiful houses, that is for sure, but the problem is you don't see the rotting interiors in some of those homes. It is easy to get caught up in the past and all the good times we had and the golden memories we encapsulate in our minds. But if we spend too much time focused on the past, we not only overlook aspects of the past that weren't so peachy keen but we often miss the present.

To have a healthy relationship with the past, we must take an objective look at our history. We do this by keeping what we hold dear—the good aspects, the things we have learned and gleaned over time—but also by unshackling ourselves from the things that left us broken and terribly scarred. One of the best techniques to do this is to take an honest look at what was, to reconsider without rose-colored lenses what is now and what you will choose to do with it all moving forward. Adolescence is a good place to start, though for some it may be wise to go earlier on the timeline. For general practice, we will begin at age twelve. In the workspace below, I invite you to open the door to yesteryear and have a little sit-down with a younger version of you. That younger you is a part of you, a layer of your personality, but there may be components of that version of you that needs healing, or perhaps a reminder of the genuine fabric of identity. Perhaps some of the aspects of you as an adolescent are of greater importance to your identity than previously thought, and they need to be reconsidered with more mature eyes and heart. For this exercise, gather some photos from old albums, yearbooks, or your mom's basement of yourself from around the ages of twelve to twenty-one (or whatever is your current age). Instead of doing this quickly, or even in one sitting, take this at a pace where you place value on little you. Give adequate attention, not just quick notice, to yourself here. You are worthy of taking the time to give focus and effort to.

Looking at the picture in your hand, place yourself back in that specific memory. What did your clothes feel like? How did the air smell around you—was it a crisp aroma of fall or maybe a brisk whiff of winter? If you had to boil it down to a few sentences, how did this version of you feel about yourself? What were the main insecurities you held within? What did you love about yourself? What was one thing you were proud of or that makes you smile knowing it was an aspect of you as a person? What was the biggest struggle you were facing, or the newest one? What was the best accomplishment of that year, or something you overcame? Take as much space on the paper as you feel led but have a real conversation with yourself at age twelve, thirteen, and so on. When you take the time to have a conversation with younger you, then you can realize the parts of the present-day you that may need a little extra love, a focus on healing, or a reemerging of something that was important to you. This can also help shed light on why you might be struggling in certain ways as an adult, or reveal aspects that you could revisit to allow more internal work to take place. This exercise is not the entire process, for there is much more to unearth, but it is a tool for discerning between the specks of dirt and the gems.

This could open the door to healing what has occurred in the past, and very likely might provoke a broader, longer conversation with a therapist, mentor, or God in prayer. In fact, I encourage you richly to invite God into this process to allow His Spirit to reveal to you what He desires you to know about each year you navigate through. This may seem like you are opening closet doors to find skeletons, but once you air out that closet you might just find the monsters never really had reason to make their home there, and it is time for them to move along. It might also instill in you a renewed love for something that once mattered greatly to you.

Let's give it a shot together below:

At age twelve I would describe myself in a word or phrase as _____.

At age twelve the biggest struggle I never told anyone about was_____.

At age twelve the biggest victory I had was_____
_____.

At age twelve the hidden or given refrain of life was

_____.

If I could give twelve-year-old me one bit of encouragement, it would be _____.

Something I would like to adopt as a ____-year-old that I did as a twelve-year-old is _____.

Something I still carry within from age twelve that I would like to no longer take with me into the future is _____.

Twelve-year-old me is worthy of _____, and ____-year-old me is worthy of the same thing.

Don't stop there. You may think of a million more ways to encourage, scold, help, weep with, root for, or offer kindness to any version of yourself. You are worthy of doing the work, and the current and future versions of you will find a lighter, brighter, healthier spirit going forward because you did the internal work of healing younger you.

STRIPPING WHAT ISN'T YOU

In gardening, one of the most important tasks is the pruning process. If you are not a botanist or your thumb lacks a greenish hue, pruning simply means the removal of dead or overgrown parts of a plant to help the plant thrive in the future. To become who you were truly meant to be, there must be a pruning process.

Let's think of it in other terms. Michelangelo, the famous artist and sculptor behind the Sistine Chapel ceiling and the David statue, offered, "The sculpture is already complete within the marble block before I start my work. It is already there; I just must chisel away the superfluous material." The same can be said of you. Somewhere inside you is the person you were meant to be, but a process is required to remove and then heal what is not you. Another term for this can be sanctification, which is the refinement that is done through the Holy Spirit to help us become more like Christ.

In considering sanctification, we can learn much from the story of how silver is refined and the process in which it comes into its intended form. I heard a sermon once on how this comes about, and the story is one we all can draw encouragement from:

"And he shall sit as a refiner and purifier of silver" (Mal. 3:3). This puzzled a Bible study group. One of the members offered to learn about the process of refining silver and inform them at their next study. He visited a silversmith and watched him at work. He watched the silversmith hold a piece of silver over the fire and let it heat up. The silversmith explained that in refining silver, you must hold the silver in the middle of the fire where the flames were hottest to burn away all the impurities. The member then thought about God holding us where the flames are the hottest to burn away our impurities. Then he thought again about the verse. "And he shall sit as a refiner and purifier of silver." He asked the silversmith if it was true that he had to sit there in front of the fire and watch the process at all times. The silversmith answered that not only did he have to sit there holding the silver, but he had to keep his eyes on the silver the entire time it was tested in the fire. If the silver was left a moment too long in the flames, it would be destroyed. You must leave it long enough to serve the purpose, but not too long as it would destroy it. The member was silent for a moment. Then he asked the silversmith, "How do you know when silver is fully refined?" He smiled and answered, "Oh, that's easy—when I see my image in it." (Author unknown)[6]

Just as with the refining of silver, the act of pruning or stripping away all that is not beneficial for you is to allow you to flourish and to encourage new growth, allowing all that has been hidden to have the space to emerge. Perhaps there are layers of the secret garden of your heart that are yet to be seen because they've been hidden behind tall weeds. Are there areas in your life where you need to let go of the weeds so that the garden can flourish and grow? Are there past hurts, resentments, or chips on your shoulder? Remember, you hold the power to clench tightly to them or to liberate yourself from Are there habits you persist in doing that you know deep down are toxic to your ecosystem? Are there aspects of your life that you fear splitting with because it would invoke severe change, even though you know that it would be not only a catharsis but a release from so much burden? You likely have something floating in your mind right now as you read these words that connects to one or more of these challenges, and I didn't even have to call it out by name.

In John 15, Jesus gives us a picture of what it means for us to be pruned by the Father's loving hand:

> I am the true vine, and my Father is the gardener. He cuts off every branch in me that bears no fruit, while every branch that does bear fruit he prunes so that it will be even more fruitful. You are already clean because of the word I have spoken to you. Remain in me, as I also remain in you. No branch can bear fruit by itself; it must remain in the vine. Neither can you bear fruit unless you remain in me.
>
> I am the vine; you are the branches. If you remain in me and I in you, you will bear much fruit; apart from me you can do nothing. If you do not remain in me, you are like a branch that is thrown away and withers; such branches are picked up, thrown into the fire and burned. If you remain in me and my words remain in you, ask whatever you wish, and it will be done for you. This is to my Father's glory, that you bear much fruit, showing yourselves to be my disciples. (John 15:1–8)

For us to bear more fruit, there will be times in which things in our life must be pruned away. This is not to punish us, nor is it to harm us; rather it is done so that we may instead enter the abundance God really has for us and be better able to accomplish what He desires for us during our lifetime here on earth. This can look different than we might expect, for at times it will not be as simple as giving up bad habits or changing a daily routine.

Maybe you have resisted giving up a social group because it seems too difficult to make new friends, even though you know the current group is harmful to your spirit. On the other hand, you may have considered a habit like endless scrolling on social media that rips your life away. It is seemingly harmless and a fast way to get some dopamine surges, but it clogs your brain and leaves your eyes and mind overstimulated. We often continue to drink from these fountains because it is what we have known for so long or because they give us some satisfaction, if even a cheap fix. Consider for a moment what it would be like if you were courageous enough to make a change in even one area, to relinquish one bad habit and pick up a better one? What if?

Put this book down for a few minutes and think about areas of your life: social, work, etc. Ask God to help you, one area at a time, to identify what the good fruit is (see Galatians 5:22,23 and Philippians 4:8), and what is dead that you are latching onto that is causing harm to your life. With what is in your control in this moment, what are one to three changes you can make to prune off something that is holding you back from a healthier existence? Ask God to reveal to your heart what should stay and what really needs to go. It does not have to be quitting a job in a detrimental workplace, unless God instructs you to do so, but make attempts somewhere small. What is one bad habit you can seek to break, or what is one shift you have the power to make that will yield results? It is not only a good idea to invite God into this process, but you really should not go at this alone, for there is Someone who knows you far better than you know yourself. He knows exactly what should stay, what should go, what should shift, and what should be acquired. God knows and through His Holy Spirit, you can experience not only this process but the gift of coming to know the Spirit of God in greater depth.

LETTING THE OLD SELF DIE

During life there is an imperative choice that is to be made: to follow Christ or to follow man. Following man yields a spirit of people-pleasing and the burnout that results from such. It produces disappointment and frustration, and it yields wearing upon your lapel all the assumptions others place on you. Is that who you really are, and is that who you really want to be during your life? What then is the alternative?

The alternative, though counter to the culture we experience daily, is to follow Christ—to surrender what you think you want and what others have told you is the way to go about things—and to be a God pleaser, not a people pleaser. Remember, you cannot serve both God and man, and as much as you try to reason that there is a third option, there is not. Jesus said to His disciples, "Whoever wants to be my disciple must deny themselves and take up their cross and follow me" (Matthew 16:24). When you deny the flesh and are reborn of the Spirit, you begin to experience life and life abundantly in the Spirit. This does not mean that you lose the fleshly rental of a body your soul currently abides in, nor does it mean you will no longer have the urges of the flesh. Rather, this is when God begins in us the process of sanctification, where He is at work conforming us to the image of Christ. Ephesians 4:22–24 tells us "to put off your old self,... and to put on the new self, created to be like God in true righteousness and holiness." What then does it mean to be the "new self" in application?

Intentional living is living with purpose. Much of intentional living looks like daily making the choice to deny the old self, deny the flesh, deny the taunts and temptations of the Enemy. Instead, we make our focus Christ, and the things in life He has given us in portion to manage, cultivate, and foster in season, and we engage in relationship. This relationship ought to be the most important one you will ever have in life—your first and best love. What is ineffably glorious is that God wants to be in relationship with us as well: "What a friend we have in Jesus." This tune sometimes seems to randomly play in my head, but I don't think it is coincidence; rather, it reminds me of that fact, and prompts me to sing in worship, praise, and gratitude.

John 10 offers us a unique perspective of this truth of knowing Christ genuinely in relationship. It blows my mind studying Scripture not only in English but in its original languages. In the Greek, John 10 encompasses two forms of "knowing." The first comes from verse 4, *eido*, which means to perceive in the way the sheep can recognize a voice. Think of it in the way that you can recognize a jingle from a commercial, even if you aren't a fan of the product. You just recognize it. The second comes vividly in verse 14: *ginosko*, to know personally, intimately, at that soul level. And that is where God knows His sheep and where they sheep not only recognize Him but really, truly *know* Him. The Lord desires that we have that *ginosko* relationship with Him, not just the *eido* one. What a friend we have in Jesus—truly, what a friend! He desires that relationship with you, but it requires action on your behalf to engage in such relationship.

Canaan Baca has a song, "More Like Jesus," that expresses how often we are told by society, culture, and those around us to "live our own truth" or live in a way entirely fueled by feelings, but how those are quickly fleeting. Chasing feelings more often than not leads us to feel excessively lost and chained to what we reason in our fleshly hearts to be correct. That is not freedom. He echoes again and again in the song the prayer,

> Holy Spirit make me more like Jesus,
> every day a little more like Jesus
> Crucify my flesh with Yours
> that my new life might be secured[7]

In denying your old self to pick up the new life in Christ, you are surrendering what you have known previously. New interests, hobbies, careers likely will emerge. In allowing God, the Author of your life, to write your story, you may find that nothing looks like it used to. However, there will be a peace that is far beyond understanding in that you are ever more becoming what God has for you, not the counterfeit version the flesh convinced you to be. Because of free will, we have the option to live in the "authorized" place of existence, where it is permitted, but is it beneficial? By choosing to live in the Authored will of God, it is there that He holds the pen, not you.

Yet isn't it an easy price for the abundance that can come from life richly abided in Christ? Many of us fret that perhaps we are too far gone, asking why God would want a relationship with us when we have run so far from Him. The beauty of such a loving heavenly Father as God is that no matter how far we have run, no matter what we have done, He wants us to come back home.

Denying the old self means growing into the new life that Christ died to give you. There you can find what Ephesians 2:22 really means: "And in him you too are being built together to become a dwelling in which God lives by his Spirit." If you still linger in fear to put away the old and experience the new, approach it with the curiosity of "what if?" and see just how God will answer.

CLEAN OUT THE CLOSET

Another facet I found in my own personal journey was the need to take a long, hard look at my closet. For me, clothing is an outward expression of my inward self, and that inward self has seen a few remodels over the years attempting to find just the right fit... literally.

Take notice of your closet. Why are you drawn to certain colors or fabrics? We wear our identities for the world to see in our clothing first and foremost, but life does not have a uniform. Proverbs 31:25 says that a woman of noble character is "clothed with strength and dignity." Let us ponder this for a moment. She adorns herself with strength, a humble confidence, that comes from God Himself. Her dignity is evident as she conducts herself. More than likely if anyone ever said a cross word about her, it would never be believed because of her dignity. In similar fashion, Isaiah 52 encourages us, "Awake, awake, Zion, clothe yourself with strength!" God has fashioned us to wear what He has uniquely designed for us. Not merely fabrics for our bodies but spiritual garments of strength, splendor, and sustaining grace.

For most of high school, I had what you could call an eclectic personal style. As I mentioned earlier, on the first day of school I had chosen an adorable, embroidered corduroy skirt with little cats on it...not everyone's preferred go-to. Looking back, I was just about fifteen years ahead of the curve with some of the more alternative styles around now, but at the time I was not received well. This was a personal style choice that was rejected by those around me, so I attempted to shift to what I thought would bring acceptance. This attempt was accepted by those around me, but I found in wearing preppy clothes that I felt like a poser—because I was. I was posing and pretending to be someone I was not.

Years later I found myself standing at my closet right before my thirtieth birthday really questioning if the items within were a true representation of the woman within. I did an extensive overhaul, but I found that nearly starting from scratch with my wardrobe was one of the best things I could have ever done for myself. Poshmark and Goodwill became assets as I let go of most of the clothing I owned. Believe me, I was not financially in a place to do a complete Extreme Closet Makeover and I lacked the backing of a *TLC* reality show for assistance, but it felt like something I was meant to do. And it was. I didn't resist this urge to refresh my closet.

It hit me about six months later when I was in an Anthropologie dressing room trying on some jeans from the clearance rack that looked kind of intriguing. I had not heard of the brand before, but the denim color was that perfect deep lunar midnight, and they were marked 75 percent off. As I slipped the jeans on and looked at myself in the mirror, I began to tear up. It was an automatic response, a nearly uncontrollable release of gratitude and joy because I finally found my look *at long last.* They fit like a dream. Suddenly my at-home high school comfort look—bootcut jeans, Chuck Taylors, and a comfortable hoodie—merged and melded with this thirty-year-old version of me into an authentic representation of the casual, comfortable, confident Cally. It wasn't that they were a nice brand, that they were on clearance, or that they were even in style; it's that they showed what I don't have to say. They showed the real me. From fit to feel,

I thought the aspects of my personality were properly exhibited in a pair of pants. I'm keeping those jeans for the long haul.

You may not have the same almost miraculous experience I did in an Anthropologie, but I do believe that if you are willing to make an adjustment in your closet, you will find existing in your own skin feels a little less itchy and a little more fun. Those jeans didn't make me lose ten pounds instantly, they didn't scrub away the jeers of other kids from fifteen years prior, and they didn't send me on some summer-long journey with my friends like in *Sisterhood of the Traveling Pants*. But what they did do is present a glimpse of the me I really want the world to see. A woman who is a little alternative in dress, but very approachable, and who is happy to just be herself.

Don't dress for your age, dress for your approach.

If you stop dressing for your age or station in life, and you instead dress for your approach toward life, you are dressing for you, not anyone else. This was painted vividly for me by my friend Karrie. She is in her mid-fifties, but she doesn't dress like the typical fifty-something mom of three. Her style is very free, boho, but it is so reflective of the spirit within. Whenever we are in public, even the softness of her flowy skirts somehow invites people to find that soft comfort in her heart and strangers seem to tell her their life stories. Her heart approach is seen physically by the clothing she wears, and it is all because she chooses to dress not how you would assume she should but for what helps her feel at peace.

Women in particular face a lot of criticism and reproach for how they dress. Depending on your figure, you are either dressing too frumpy or too sexy or too basic, but at the end of the day we can choose whether to adopt the opinions of others or to let them slide off our backs. My own personal approach is to wear a dress fitted enough to show I am a woman, but loose enough to show I am a lady. Remember too that your own inner attitude, confidence, and intention will shine through in *how* you wear an outfit. Every girl at the ball in *Cinderella* had a beautiful gown that night, but only Cinderella stood out. She wasn't afraid of letting the heart of courage and kindness shine through her, and you shouldn't be either. Dress for your approach toward life, not your age or the views of others.

One practical way you can overhaul your closet and find your "approach look" can be simply to ask yourself, if you saw that item on another person, what words, phrases, or connotations would come to mind? Would you consider that item to be in the realm of who you want to reflect to the world? Does that item make you feel joy, or does it make you feel at odds within yourself? Is the item something you want to be a symbolic piece of your demeanor and a reflection of who you are? This process is likely something you will not do all in one night, but there is a huge catharsis when you enter a closet specifically tailored to the one-of-a-kind you.

CONTENTMENT VS. APATHY

I used to question if contentment was something one could truly experience, or if it was a softer, lacier, more comfortable way of saying you were apathetic. I'll admit I am the first to be a paradoxical creature of so much optimism within while wearing a pair of cynical spectacles I often choose to see the world through. Contentment in any area of life seemed like such a foreign concept, and even with my great imagination its existence seemed to be a farce. The answer came in like a leaf maturing into its autumn colors, slowly but then fully.

The thing about transitions is, in the moment, we rarely recognize them happening. It feels like more of the same wait until we look back and notice that change was occurring—even if it was slow to come about. The answer to the question of contentment came in a similar way, perhaps because I released it from being a constant thought and thread of curiosity I would tug on. I stopped pulling at the threads of what I was hoping for in the future and instead I just let them be. Learning to live in the moment and to richly soak in the present and the glorious gift it all is became my focus rather than what my aching heart longed for and lacked. Somewhere along the way, not in a single breath or movement, I found that there is so much to behold in the now. This moment you are currently in will never exist again but in memory, and squandering the present hyper-focused on the future is futile—a waste of your time, energy, and potential. There was also the sense that finding contentment in the present moment did not mean a dream has died, or that that it no longer was held it in the locket of one's heart. It did not mean that it was no longer a desire, but it meant there wasn't a missing out in the abundance of today.

We always want to "skip to the good part," but we need to realize we are *in* the good part. There are things in the past that you would consider the good parts of life that in the moment you didn't realize you might one day lose. Some of these things are so minuscule or commonplace that we don't even consider them aspects of life that could be lost. I think that is why there is such a deep-seated desire to dig up nostalgia. "Nostalgia" is from the Greek words *nostos* ("return" or "homecoming") and *algos* ("suffering" or "pain"). So nostalgia is the suffering caused by an unappeased yearning to return. Nostalgia for many of us is longing to return to a place or time, but there is a suffering we experience while longing for that life again. That raises some questions: Where are the physical places or particular events that we might one day find ourselves nostalgic about? Would we be as inclined toward nostalgia if we thoroughly and thoughtfully abided in the present? That feeling of excitement on a Friday night—grabbing the last VHS new release and a bucket of popcorn and enjoying the simplicity of life—is now gone forever with unlimited access to streaming services without leaving your couch.

Life doesn't need to be perfect to be good, and there is good to find in this season and this day. So, ask yourself:

What is one good thing I have today that I would have craved in a former season, or I'll miss in a later season?

Allow yourself today to cherish the gift that life is, and know it doesn't negate what you long for; instead it's enjoying what you have with a grateful heart. Having gratitude in the present does not mean you don't welcome what you're longing for when it emerges in the future. It does not create a barrier for goodness to come. A heart that is thankful for what you have now is a heart lapping up all the goodness that can exist with having little, for he who can be content and a good steward of little can be entrusted with more. Contentment is a grateful heart, not a numb one.

PERSONAL REFLECTION
AND APPLICATION QUESTIONS

1. Identify one or more words that have been weaponized against you that you would like to redefine now.

2. What age did you find was the most pertinent in your development, from adolescence into adulthood?

3. What is something in you that you sense God wanting to prune?

4. If you were to design or choose one item to be reflective of your true style, what would it look like?

5. Can you feel gratitude toward one or more areas in your life where in the past you would have had a feeling of apathy?

CHAPTER 5

The Budding

If a man does not keep pace with his companions,
perhaps it is because he hears a different drummer.
Let him step to the music which he hears,
however measured or far away.
—Henry David Thoreau

Forgiveness is not an occasional act;
it is a permanent attitude.
—Martin Luther King Jr.

INNER HEALING

A few years ago, I was perusing a yard sale when I found an old-fashioned hard suitcase and knew I just had to have it. I began storing items in it like a hope chest to one day give to my future husband. My joke is that it will be the only baggage I bring into marriage. I laugh at that because it is a lofty goal, but in truth it is an earnest hope in prayer. Baggage has become something that we are all so used to carrying that we have forgotten what it would be like to not carry it around. Truly, it has become a high idealism to believe we could ever truly unpack it all and leave it behind. The question remains: does that baggage define us? Does that baggage hold a claim ticket to who we truly are, or can it be worked through?

Even those with the most picturesque lives have seen a downturn at some point or another. There is not a single person on this earth who has not experienced some kind of hardship, and much of the relatable traumas we endure can be bonding experiences to share. What is important to hold firm to is that we are not what has happened to us. These things have shaped us and refined us, but they do not define us. If you lost a loved one, if you have been abused, or if you have been depressed, you are not those things. You are not loss, you are not abuse, and you are not depression. You have been touched by those events and you have been changed by those events, but you are not that sole event. You are so much more dynamic than that.

Something that never seems to occur to us, though it is so obvious, is that we can unpack that baggage. Now, opening baggage after a long and enduring trip will rarely be tidy, but it is possible. It is possible to look at each item, acknowledge it, and move forward on your journey. So, let's get started.

UNPACKING LIST

It is easier to sort through the smaller stuff first. These are like chips we've held on our shoulders. They weigh us down but they don't tip the scales.

Toiletry bag: Typically, you place small cover-up items in here: makeup, Band-Aids, salves that cover up the hurt. These are the masks we use to hide our pain—our coping mechanisms. If we are truly going to unpack our lives, our hurts, and our baggage, then we need to throw these things out the window and come into the real, authentic, raw, and honest parts of ourselves.

Shoes: These boots are made for walking, and that's just what they'll do. The shoe items are things we can walk away from more easily than not. These hurts and pains are like chips on our shoulders, petty grudges, or things that we hold on to and really should release. Perhaps a time you were cheated out of a job that fostered resentment toward a company or a boss. Maybe there was an event that you were skipped over for or not invited to. These are things that hurt at the time, but they are in the past, not the present. We can choose to let go of them and walk away.

Heavy coat: Heavy coats represent heavy and deep pains. This could be the loss of something, or someone, extremely important to us. This could be the pain incited from a very deep and scarring season of depression. These coats weigh us down daily. They heat us to the point of stifling even new seasons. If we are to walk into the spring of a new life of identity, we must put away the heavy coats of winters past. The dark and desolate days of your life have passed, and it is time to move on to the newness of spring. Spring does not require carrying a heavy coat anymore.

Shirts: Shirts represent the most vulnerable of all our baggage. They cover our nakedness, the highest levels of shame and rawness we carry. For many, these shirts have manifested as cutting, self-harm, or eating disorders. They cover the deepest pains of abuse, loss, and devastation. In the next section, we will discuss how to truly put away these shirts for good, but for now it is vital we recognize them. It takes confronting the monster to truly defeat it once and for all and to walk forward in true freedom.

Before turning the page, I encourage you to list your baggage. This book is meant to be an interactive study in self-awareness. Keep the list between you and your Creator but list these truths. For when we see them in plain sight, we can know how to handle them correctly.

DO YOU WANT TO BE HEALED?

Do you believe you can be healed? Don't just gloss over this question; I'm literally asking you, "Do you believe you can be healed?" Regardless of the answer to that question, do you *want* to be healed? Jesus asked this of a man near a pool in Bethesda. The day unfolds:

> Some time later, Jesus went up to Jerusalem for one of the Jewish festivals. Now there is in Jerusalem near

the Sheep Gate a pool, which in Aramaic is called Bethesda and which is surrounded by five covered colonnades. Here a great number of disabled people used to lie—the blind, the lame, the paralyzed. One who was there had been an invalid for thirty-eight years. When Jesus saw him lying there and learned that he had been in this condition for a long time, he asked him, "Do you want to get well?"

"Sir," the invalid replied, "I have no one to help me into the pool when the water is stirred. While I am trying to get in, someone else goes down ahead of me."

Then Jesus said to him, "Get up! Pick up your mat and walk." At once the man was cured; he picked up his mat and walked. (John 5:1–9)

Let's not just take this at face value; let's dissect it as much as we can for fuller comprehension. It was more than obvious to Jesus that the man was disabled. The Pool of Bethesda was a modern-day type of nursing home. People would go and lay around this pool just waiting for water to bubble up, because they believed the water held healing powers.

The first thing I think of here is Lieutenant Dan in *Forrest Gump*. He was a man who built his identity on being a lieutenant in the US Army. Both he and Forest had been wounded in the Vietnam War, but Lieutenant Dan had lost both of his legs. Forest, who had only endured a minor wound, went to visit his old friend. A spirit of resentment and bitterness had come over Dan. He respected his family's legacy of men who died fighting for their country, so in his eyes surviving was worse than death. No longer having legs, he felt that he had been sentenced to prison in merely surviving. Dan sat among men in similar condition, but he was exhausted and defeated within. I imagine the man Jesus went to see that day at the Pool to be much like Lieutenant Dan.

Let's consider again how the story unfolds. As Jesus asked if he wanted to get well, the invalid replied, "Sir, I have no one to help me." The man felt defeated before he even tried. He was wallowing in his despair that he had failed before he even tried. You could say that "he's learned to slam on the brake, before he's even turned the key" (*Dear Evan Hanson*). With all this said, Jesus does not merely snap His fingers and provide a healing. He inquires to see if the man wants to be healed. Why would He do this? James 4:2 hits hard:

> You want what you don't have, so you scheme and kill to get it. You are jealous of what others have, but you can't get it, so you fight and wage war to take it away from them. Yet you don't have what you want because you don't ask God for it. (NLT)

We do not have because we do not ask. It is not that God cannot heal; it is that we need to ask.

Not only do we need to ask, but we need to be willing to believe that He can and will heal us. Stay with me here. C. S. Lewis once wisely stated, "We are not necessarily doubting that God will do the best for us; we are wondering how painful the best will turn out to be." We may have full faith that He can do it, but just as we found in the baggage chapter, unpacking all that mess can be chaotic and painful. The question remains: *what if?* What if we asked Him to heal us? What if we let Him into those dark places? What if we gave Him full access to the closets with all our skeletons? What if?

Inner Healing: A Handbook for Helping Yourself and Others by Mike Flynn and Doug Gregg offers an interesting approach toward healing, including my own journey. This book shifted my perspective as to how one can go about digging up what is beneath the surface to be healed. The truth is that God not only can, but He wants to come in and heal. He wants to pour His Light into the darkness of our hearts. Healing is real, and healing is possible. I encourage you to begin with a very simple prayer:

> Dear Lord, I believe You can heal me... and Jesus, I want to be healed. I want You to come into my situation and heal me. These memories haunt me, they taunt me from moving forward in life. I know You intended more for me, and I know I want more for my life than this. Would You heal me? In Jesus' name, Amen.

The man at the Pool of Bethesda was not the only one Jesus healed in such a uniquely told way. John 9 details the story of a man who was born blind. Jesus heals him, but the question is asked if he was the one who had sinned or his parents. This implies that somehow he had brought the blindness upon himself. Jesus replies to their questions and shares something vital: "This happened so the power of God could be seen in him" (v. 3, NLT). Through this man's healing, others would see. Perhaps the same can be said for us. Through the healing of wounds or infirmities that we would never have expected to be healed, others would be inspired to seek Jesus for themselves. Our own healed wounds and experiences serve as points of connection with others, and being able to use the wisdom we gain to help someone else get through the process is invaluable.

Healing in the Bible is not limited to just physical healing. In 2 Kings 6 we read, "O LORD, open his eyes and let him see!" (NLT). In this story, Elisha is praying for another to see what God had shown him. In the same way, when we ask for healing and He chooses to heal us, others will see the change. They will see that you no longer carry the burden or baggage of the past, and they will see the freedom that comes from being healed by Christ. Not only that, but you too will be so free and light that you will desire to tell anyone and everyone you can of your great healing. Invite Him into healing whatever you are carrying. Invite Him to wipe away that pain and move forward into the freedom of your identity.

FORGIVENESS

I would be remiss if we did not discuss that there is a very pertinent need for forgiveness in the journey toward blooming. In several ways, forgiveness is less about what has occurred or even about the one who invoked the hurt—it's about you. It's about the wounds, the scars, the aftereffects that you carry within, and the things that haunt you. It's opening the closet door of your heart at times to find a staircase to the catacombs of your innermost being. Those tunnels may be stricken with gullies of darkness and cobwebs of memory, but how much better would it be if you let the light in to those delicate places? Forgiveness is the key to the gates of freedom.

An aspect of forgiveness is recognizing that the other person may never acknowledge or accept that they have wronged you. Ephesians 4:32 reminds us, "Be kind and compassionate to one another, forgiving each other, just as in Christ God forgave you." It is all right to fully realize that, although it may not have been their intention to harm you, it is your reality that you live with, a reality you endure. Their validation is not required for your healing process, nor is it required for forgiveness to be given to them. Forgiveness is something you offer in your own mind, heart, or spirit releasing you from that connection.

Forgiveness between humans does not mean that you must allow that person back into your life either. It very often can mean that you allow them to interact with you and in some cases have a seat at your table again, but it does not mean that you have to go back to the way things were before. You have acquired wisdom moving forward with them, and you retain that wisdom and knowledge of whether trust is in the process of rebuilding, is rebuild, or is without repair. Whichever category the relationship falls into is between you and God, and at times with the assistance of a therapist. You have learned from an experience in order that you do not have to endure it again, so apply what you have learned moving forward regarding the other person(s).

There is an aspect of forgiveness as well in accepting people the way they are. Many of us carry soul wounds from family members and for the life of us cannot fathom why they would act in such a way, or why they do not seek to learn and change. You cannot control the actions of others, but you can control your response and how you accept their actions.

Think about it in this way: If you expect someone who speaks only Spanish to speak to you in English, you are going to be very frustrated and confused when the only words that come out of their mouth are in Spanish. You can hope and hope and hope that one day they'll open their mouth and they'll suddenly be speaking your native language of English, but unless they make the choice to learn English that is not going to happen. As hard as it is, stop expecting them to speak your language. To take it the extra mile, see what it means to learn their language of Spanish to see if through empathy and effort you can come to understand what they are saying. It doesn't mean it will match your own heart's native language, but it can provide a bridge of understanding. Our hearts all speak different languages, meaning how you receive a statement may differ from how someone else receives it, but it is on you if you choose to learn another language or not. It is also on you what your expectations are regarding how others speak and communicate.

Lastly, forgiveness of self is an aspect of the blooming. There are things you have done in the past to yourself or to others that you cannot undo. As nice as it would be, very few of us own a flux capacitor (the time machine from *Back to the Future*) with the ability to return to another time to undo a mistake before it happens. You may have to live with the consequences of your mistakes, but you do not have to live with the self-condemnation of those mistakes. Even without the forgiveness of other people, you can forgive yourself for the things you have done. You can make the choice not to repeat them again, and to seek out getting help if necessary. It is possible to change, and that change begins with Christ. When Christ called Saul from his life of terrorizing and persecuting Christians into a new life as Paul to minister on Jesus' behalf, we see true, authentic change. There was a journey that led to that change, but Paul did in fact change and his life was moved in such a dramatic way that it was evident that change was authored by God.

In that vein, don't hold against yourself the things you did as another version of you. Paul remembered his past only in the way that he did not wish to return to that version of himself, rather he wanted to live as the new man God made him to be. Forgive that former version of yourself and help the person you are becoming to grow into someone who would not actively choose to make that mistake again. Choose to be the better you and extend to yourself the kind of grace you are willing to give to others. Consider Paul's perspective in 1 Timothy 1:12–14:

I thank Christ Jesus our Lord, who has given me strength, that he considered me trustworthy, appointing me to his service. Even though I was once a blasphemer and a persecutor and a violent man, I was shown mercy because I acted in ignorance and unbelief. The grace of our Lord was poured out on me abundantly, along with the faith and love that are in Christ Jesus.

Forgiveness in any form is a journey and not one that is quick. It can look like choosing daily to render forgiveness, and some days that is harder than others. The important thing is that you take the first step forward in whatever that looks like for the situation, because at the end of the day the one who really finds freedom is you.

EYE OF THE BEHOLDER

An exquisite aspect of humans lies in the fact that each of us has a different preference when it comes to just about anything. From colors to flowers to career, the answer to one's choice will vary. That does not mean one flower is fairer than another; rather, there is not one specific flower that is everyone's favorite. Why else would Baskin-Robbins need to have thirty-one (and counting!) flavors if everyone would always choose chocolate?

You may not be everyone's cup of tea, their favorite flower, or their go-to ice cream flavor, and there is nothing wrong with that. It does not strip away your significance or desirability. Someone once quipped that if we do not find ourselves attractive, it is not that we are ugly; it's just that you aren't your own type. It does not mean that you are not the type for someone else. There is nothing wrong with being an acquired taste; if anything, it's kind of a compliment. What a rarity you are for the refined palate.

If beauty is really in the eye of the beholder, that concept can find itself applicable in other areas, including the acceptance of self. What qualities do you find particularly admirable, lovely, or beautiful? Write them down. Perhaps you thought of someone who is honest, yet kind in how they present a hard truth. I like to say that if you must present a truth that is a hard pill to swallow, wrap it in some cheese to help it go down easier. It does not mean the truth is not embedded, potent, and fully there, but it is given in such a way that it is a little more manageable to consume. If instead of keeping your mouth shut or offering a little white lie when someone asks your opinion, what if you determined to be someone who offered truth? Would there not be a beauty that would pour out from doing such an action? Don't just appreciate beauty in your own eyes from others; cultivate a life in which you live by the same principles and actions yourself.

If optimism is not natural to you, but you see the benefits and fruit that can come from an optimistic point of view, how can you rewire your brain? One way is to find even the smallest grain of anything good during a cluster of a mess. For this one I like to say, "At least there's one M&M in your trail mix," which basically means in all the nuts and raisins life will hand you in a package, maybe, just maybe, you can find one little sweet something to remark on in a positive light. It may not be your second nature and it may not be something you have been shown properly in formative years, but it is something you can embrace in your life now to take forward. You aren't a slab of concrete unable to change; you are a piece of clay that is continuously being molded. Isaiah 64:8 reminds us, "Yet you, LORD, are our Father. We are the clay, you are the potter; we are all the work of your hand." You are being molded and shaped as you live your life following Him and obeying Him. This is not the you who always was, but the person you can be with His molding and shaping into all you can become.

What about the exteriors of life? Can a beautiful life look different from how most people live life? One of the most common insecurities I have heard whispered in vulnerability is when someone is operating in a way that is not the norm for most. Perhaps you have chosen for your family that the best option is for the mother to stay at home and raise the kids instead of getting a full-time job and placing the children in daycare. This is how it was done for thousands of years, but in recent decades the way things were done has shifted and the idea of mom working full-time has become the typical way of doing things. Many moms have shared that if they don't have a full-time career outside of the home, they feel self-conscious and like others think they are lazy or that they don't add anything to the world. What a horrible lie they have bought into, thinking they are only worth what they can produce by means of money or a run-of-the-mill career.

As if raising a child is not a job! Choosing to live in a way that is not the typical can feel awkward, but remember that you are the one who must live the day to day. What is the right fit for one may not be the right fit for another, but what a gift it is to live in a time and age where there is the freedom to find the custom fit for you.

Custom fits can vary, and they should! To wrap around to Ricky Nelson's quip, "You can't please everyone." Don't live for the affirmation of other people. Do what is right for your family, for you, and for the life you have been given to live.

Beauty is in the eye of the beholder, so as the beholder, what forms of beauty do you want to cultivate in and around you? Start with inward qualities and allow them to trickle out into a life that is without question something you find breathtakingly winsome and alluring.

PICK ME GIRLS

A "pick me girl" is a flower hoping to be chosen and picked. She likely would be someone who would selectively and sequentially pluck petals off a flower to determine if "he likes me, he likes me not." She's someone who is insecure and is looking for outward validation and, in an effort to receive such validation, she behaves in a way to receive attention. "Pick me girls" need to pick themselves.

You don't have to wait for someone to pick you before you can choose yourself. More importantly you can remember that God has chosen you. This is not dependent upon another human being to make the conscience effort to do the same in choosing you. It's a common thread that finds itself running through a spectrum of story lines. From movies to books to the actuality of lives, many find themselves wanting to be wanted, desiring to be desired, and desperate to be seen, known, and loved. At the end of the day, isn't that the deep wish of every human heart?

To be fully known, fully seen, and fully loved is something that almost seems fully unattainable, but the fullest truth of all is that it can be so. God already knows every single thing about you, and it is His pleasure to accept you, love you, and welcome you into His Garden. We have the choice to pick Him too—to acknowledge Jesus as our Savior—and that is a decision that only you can make for yourself; no one else can pick Him for you.

Choosing or picking yourself is not a case where you are selfishly and constantly putting yourself first; rather, it is making careful considerations and decisions in which the consequences are honoring to those around you and to you. Your name is not "Doormat," so stop living like it is.

Picking yourself also means caring for the vessel your soul abides in, your fleshly body. It means caring for it as you would a precious commodity that you get only one of in this lifetime. Since you cannot get a body transplant and you cannot swap your body for a newer model, the one you are operating in deserves care and upkeep. That's why caring for the body you are in is so vital. You cannot exist in another body, so part of honoring yourself is caring for that rental your soul abides in on earth.

Picking yourself also looks like discerning what is fair to you. Life is not fair and there will always be a circumstance or time when you do get the short end of the stick, but that is not the constant and enduring portion of your life. You can stand up for yourself, speak up for yourself, and courageously step up for yourself so that you are not always placed at the bottom of the totem pole. It is okay to pick yourself.

Human love also means loving and choosing others in such a way that you would want to be as well. It's the Golden Rule, and it is golden because it is something of great value and is precious. If you want to be loved, love others well. Do it in such a way that you do not expect anything in return. Learning to love others well is also learning the distinct way they understand, give, and receive love.

In the past it appeared that there were only five love languages, but are there really? Are we that simple that our most important emotion can be boiled down to five main types of expression? Or are there myriad very distinct and intimate ways that a dynamic human feels and expresses love? I would say the latter. It is far easier to compartmentalize love into five categories, but what if you are seeking to love someone who does not fit a mold so easily? What if you yourself do not conform to a one-size-fits-most type of love language? What if that is something that is unique and not a bad thing?

Take a moment to consider the ways that you most often feel loved or cherished. Ask God what your love language really is. Then take the word He gives or reveals through a Scripture verse and consider whether it applies to times when you felt the most loved. You might find it's not one of the five listed in *The Five Love Languages*. For example, you might personally be given the word "remembered," and find the proof is really in the pudding. Imagine that someone remembers you love white chocolate and gets you a 75-cent chocolate bar. More than likely it would mean more than if someone gave you a fifty dollar gift card to a random store. The value of the gift to you was not its monetary worth, but that the other person took time to consider you and remember a seemingly forgettable facet that makes you *you*. In the same way, offering a recollection of something subtle about you could help you to feel seen and known. If you really want to love someone, learn what makes them feel loved and cherished by discovering the way they feel seen, known, and desired. It does not have to be a singular way, but it can extend to a very tender place in a heart when that right chord is plucked.

So, how can you pick yourself today and how can you pick someone that matters to you? How can you make an effort to regard yourself and those around you highly and with honor and care because all are worthy of being chosen and loved? Lovely flowers deserve to be picked, even if that first comes from oneself.

PERSONAL REFLECTION
AND APPLICATION QUESTIONS

1. Where do you need to forgive a younger version of yourself? What grace can you offer that younger you?

2. What qualities in your opinion make someone incessantly beautiful?

3. What is one way you can pick yourself today? What is one way you can help someone else to feel chosen?

CHAPTER 6

The Blossoms

Be devoted to one another in love.
Honor one another above yourselves.
—Romans 12:10

The secret, Alice, is to surround yourself
with people who make your heart smile.
It's then, only then, that you'll find Wonderland.
—Lewis Carroll, *Alice in Wonderland*

USE YOUR VOICE

Slang is such a fascinating aspect of culture and language. In recent years, one slang phrase has been the idea of staying "on brand." Originally a marketing phrase applied to businesses, this means that habits, actions, clothing, or just about anything would be fitting and corresponding to a person. It is a unique way of offering a compliment to someone that they are remaining faithful and devoted to who they are. We all would do well to embrace the idea of staying "on brand" in more areas than just one.

For most people, social media has become the main method of interaction with one another. From sharing vacation photos to life updates, it is more efficient than any town crier ever was. Yet there is a wrench thrown in, in that there is an unspoken challenge in social media to only share what is "Insta worthy"—suitable for posting on Instagram. In using any social media account, you have a platform; you have an audience and a place to share not only with your community, but with the world the message you want to share. Use your voice for more than just the bare minimum.

Staying on brand and true to oneself while using social media platforms as a soapbox of sorts means moving past posting only what is aesthetically posed, algorithm targeted, or bait for "likes." Instead, you offer to your corner of the world the veritable you, not a facade. It strips the veneers off of social media and invites and welcomes actual connection, conversation, and community. What a beautiful way to use the voice you have in the world.

In the show *Boy Meets World*, the final episode of the series included a monologue of wisdom from the beloved teacher, Mr. Feeney. For a mainstream program it was incredible how much *Boy Meets World* sought to integrate good morals and even some biblical ideas throughout the series. In one of the final scenes, the former students ask for one more nugget of wisdom before they venture on to new pastures, and Mr. Feeney tells them to "do good."

Mr. Feeney was known for his use of proper language and semantics, so the former students meet him with confusion as to why he did not say to "do well," but he explains with a great heart of love that he wants them to go out into the world to seek to "do good." Each of us has that same opportunity even if we think we have but a whisper of a voice in this world.

As a unique individual, you leave an irreplaceable mark upon those you meet. It cannot be replicated by anyone else, nor can it be forgotten. Even if they do not remember your name, how you made them feel will be remembered. Consider that in the way you interact in real life and on social media, for it is possible to use your voice and to "do good."

STUCK ON A LEVEL

Life is a process and a journey. That is not a new concept by any means, but with such a truth comes the reality that often we can feel quite stuck. Perhaps you feel as if you are living in a video game of sorts, and you cannot seem to move past a level. Try as you might you are continuously striving to advance to the next part, and to your chagrin in the final leap onward your efforts are thwarted. Life can often leave us feeling in such a place that we are at the last second blocked; but what if there was a greater purpose we do not see?

Perspective shifts can help us when we feel stuck. It does not change the environment around us, but what it can do is help us to realize that maybe what is happening isn't happening *to you* but is happening *for you*. Think of it in another way. Instead of asking, "Why me, God?" in your current situation, ask the question, "What is God teaching me and what am I learning that I could not learn in any other way but this?" It doesn't fix the issue, it doesn't make the problem disappear, and it doesn't invalidate your feelings, but it can help you see that there is more happening than just what you can see right in this moment.

You are not an NPC (non-playable character) wandering around repeating the same phrase or action on loop in a video game. You are a dynamic, purpose-filled person brimming with destiny. Even in the seasons of life where everything feels mundane and monotonous, it doesn't mean that somehow you missed the boat, or that God has forgotten you, when in fact there could be far more happening behind the scenes than you even realize or recognize. John Piper puts it this way: "God is always doing 10,000 things in your life, and you may be aware of three of them." Think of it in the way of a plant growing. When you plant a seed, you water it, and you allow it to have sunshine, you know not to expect it to sprout right away. Weeks go by and all you can see from the surface is dirt. It takes a lot of dirt time before the sprout begins to peek its way upward, but what you don't see is all that is happening beneath the surface. Roots are stretching out to find room to spread, new root systems are forming, and all that is necessary for the plant to have a proper footing to withstand its destiny up top is growing just beneath the surface. Are we really all that different from the plants in this way?

It's amazing how the things we count as useless or a waste of time can be where skill sets are formed. Even with the video game analogy, you cannot advance to the next level until you defeat the one you are on. This is because in that next level you need to have first mastered all the challenges on the previous levels so that when it comes to executing those abilities in action you have them covered.

When I was ten years old, my mother taught me how to sew both on a sewing machine and by hand. Her sewing machine had been one of the first items she purchased as a newlywed back in 1985. By the time she was teaching me, the machine was already fifteen years old and was prone to malfunctioning. As I attempted to sew a beginner's project—a pink and white poncho—the machine went kaput with the bobbin all wound up with thread and a *screeeeetch* when I pressed the pedal again and again only to have a paralyzed needle. Instead of fixing it herself and making it easy on me, my mom had me learn how to fix the machine. She showed me how to repair the machine the first time, but with every resurgence of an issue she had me figure it out. I remember sitting, well, stewing, because she would not let me leave the dining room table until I had repaired the issue. Ten-year-old me was so annoyed that I couldn't leave the project or that she wouldn't just do it for me, but I was trained by tinkering, trying, and testing different methods to be able to advance.

Years later I took a teaching job at a small country school in which I taught US History and Home Economics. For the Home Economics course, which included teaching the children to sew, every machine the school owned had been donated. As you can imagine, these used machines were full of flaws. I remember calling my mother to thank her that she didn't let me do things the easy way fifteen years earlier. Had I not learned how to service a sewing machine as a child, I would have been up a creek without a paddle years later as a teacher. What I counted a useless and stupid task given to me by my mother when I was ten would prove a vital ability at age twenty-five in the role I had professionally. You never know what will come in handy down the road.

As difficult as it is to feel stuck on a level or in a season, ask yourself what you are learning, collecting, or gleaning in the meantime. Though these revelations are often observed in hindsight, there are times that in taking a moment to ponder what is happening, we can see that it all serves a purpose and something is being acquired even in the most ordinary of times.

THE GARDEN AROUND YOU

What does the garden around you look like? Who are the people surrounding you, and are they flowers that add to the beauty around you, or are they pernicious weeds sucking the nutrients out from the ground around you in ways you may not be aware of? Is your community an instrumental or invasive species?

Some friends are seasonal blooms in our lives, and others are meant for the long haul and find themselves in evergreen relationships. It's been said that there's a season and a reason for all relationships, and this is especially true for community. Those you surround yourself with do have an impact on the person you become and how you live your life. If you are with those who build you up, challenge you in healthy ways, and foster creativity and light, you are more likely to grow in this way. On the other hand, if you are in a flowerbed with those who drain you, take from you in the way of time and energy, and cast a pessimistic raincloud of emotion, you are not going to thrive as you potentially could. How do we know the difference between the two?

Much of this comes in the way of using wisdom and discernment. Take a moment to consider what a particular individual adds to or consumes from your life. Everyone has an off day or time in their life, but what impact does the individual have on your life overall? Is the relationship one you should continue to invest in, or is ultimately not a healthy relationship that you should engage in? Much of this realization can come when you find yourself in a predicament or a difficult season. Do those around you help you and pray for you, or are they a fair-weather friend?

I certainly encourage you to invite God into the human relationships you keep. It's biblical to do so, and it really does have an effect. First Corinthians 15:33 reminds us, "Do not be deceived: 'Bad company corrupts good morals'" (NASB). A potent prayer is one where you ask God to pluck out anyone He does not desire for you to have in your life. You would be amazed how quickly that prayer will be answered and often in ways you would not expect with people and you would not expect. In the same way, asking God to plant those He does desire for you to have in your life will yield a similar harvest. You will see new connections and relationships forming in which you have a very healthy give-and-take connection. There is also an underlying peace that comes when you invite God to plant the garden, because you know that there is a purpose, plan, and protected atmosphere with the associations in your life.

It is also important to realize that even some of the most impactful people we encounter can have but a short time in our lives. As feeling people, it can hurt when we lose a once very valued companion, but it helps to know there is a specific timing and purpose for all things (Ecclesiastes 3:1). I discovered this very vivid truth regarding a friend I considered truly thicker than blood, a closer-than-a-sister kind of friend. We were thick as thieves and often compared our friendship to that of David and Jonathan in the Bible, close and kindred, but that friendship came to a staggeringly painful halt. At first I was insanely confused, as it seemed we had such an evergreen friendship, one that was building up in godly ways and in positive aspects, but then it found itself beyond repair. After the initial blow of the friendship ending, I was able to come before God and vulnerably ask, "Why?"

The answer I was given was in the form of a metaphor. She had a seat at the metaphorical table of my life, but she occupied more than just one seat; she was so involved that it was as if she were partly reclining on the table. There was not any room whatsoever for anyone else to take a seat because she took up so much space. It was clear in that imagery that God wanted to bring in others to the table, but that was not an option if she occupied such a large space. Because of her personality, it was not possible for her to lessen her involvement in my life, so it was correct and fitting with the greater plan of God that she be dismissed from my life. She served a reason for a season, and when it was done it was done. This did not mean I did not greatly grieve the loss of someone who had become like a sister to me, but it did give me the ability to let her go and move onward.

It is important to choose friends who earnestly are for you in this life. Someone being for you has a double meaning in that they are genuinely rooting *for you*, supporting you as a person, and hoping to see your success, but it also means that they are someone God has intended *for you* in your life. When it comes to relationships, God will often bring someone in for a reason or a season, and that is why it is important that we allow all relationships in our lives to be surrendered to His hand and guidance. Many times, someone who has walked with you in your life for several years may be seated further down the table and you question why this is, but know God often moves people for a purpose in season. Connect with God and be intentional in each one of these relationships, so that you are not clinging on to someone He does not want you to or letting someone slip away when He has more in the future for your journey together.

Also take note whether those around you are lifting you up, speaking life into you, and offering you even rebuke in love. Psalm 141:5 reminds us that the rebuke of a righteous man is a gift: "Let the godly strike me! It will be a kindness! If they correct me, it is soothing medicine. Don't let me refuse it" (NLT). Of course, we hope that such rebuke will be given with consideration and in a kind way, but those who are truly for you will not enable you to continue down a bad path. Those who are for you will offer godly rebuke when they feel necessary, and it is something to take into consideration. Ask God to make it clear who He has for you in your life for this season. It may surprise you.

Know that the garden you are planted in can have a direct result in the fruit you bear and the harvest that will come in your life, so don't take it lightly when you consider your friendships and close connections.

HEALTHY CONFIDENCE VS. PRIDEFUL ARROGANCE

Much of the flourishing that can come through having self-esteem and living out what it means to be wonderfully you involves developing a healthy confidence. This is not to be confused with a prideful arrogance; rather, it is the cultivating of a healthy confidence and self-concept rooted in love of yourself as a child of God and the life He has given you to live.

There is a stark difference between cocky pride and thriving confidence. Self-esteem in its blooming form is not arrogance but the healthy fulfillment of confidently enjoying who you are and why you were placed on this planet. It is rooted in expressing why you are here in this moment on this day in this time period. Confidence is securely standing as you are without the need for the approval of others and being okay if not everyone likes you. Think of Fraulein Maria walking to the von Trapp home in *The Sound of Music* as she sang "I Have Confidence." Sometimes a little pep talk (or song) can go a long way. And truly at the end of the day, if God likes you, that's what matters. You like you, and that matters. It involves recognizing the great gift it is to not only be alive but to get to be you. Consider how no one else on this planet gets to do the things you do or live the life you live. When we reframe our mindset to be that I "get to" live this life, not I "have to" live this life, we begin to see that our lives are a wonderful adventure that we are privileged to walk out daily. That reframing of the mind can be a difficult challenge for those who struggle with depression, anxiety, or other hard realities in life.

For those who battle the darkness, the concept of being wonderfully alive sounds almost like a fairy tale, something of make-believe. Yet there is a challenge embedded with that: if, instead of caving to the depression and the darkness, you approach life with gratitude, not an obligation to live, perhaps in time existing becomes truly living. You stop merely existing when you approach life as something to be grateful for, not as a forced task. N. T. Wright offers the inspiration, "When you gaze in love and gratitude at the God in whose image you were made, you do indeed grow. You discover more of what it means to be fully alive." You begin to live, and live abundantly, when you see that it's an honor to be on this planet at this very time in history and you get to be you. No one else has the ideas you have, and no one else gets to do some of the one-of-a-kind opportunities you get to. Even if you feel you have the most boring or lackluster of lives, you must concede that you have been given certain opportunities that others have not. Consider even one story you'd tell someone of an experience you lived out, something you got to do that few could say the same of.

There is a scene in the 2005 movie *Walk the Line* where Johnny Cash was playing a set of songs and was met with an intriguing question by his producer: If he was lying in a ditch about to die and could sing one final ode, one final swan song, what would he sing? Cash answered, "Folsom Prison Blues." What song would you play? What would your story be if you could tell one story from your life? What is something you have seen or known that no one else has, or that a select few could share?

Part of building up one's confidence is allowing yourself to love you too. Loving yourself does not mean that you suddenly adopt a Narcissus-level view of yourself, or that you somehow place yourself as an idol or deity upon a pedestal. It means that you peel back the layers of all that others have imposed upon you, and all that is false and said by the Enemy, and you fully and radically embrace with a robust joy all that is you and who God says you are and let yourself love it.

Consider the things you love about others and how in loving those qualities you are not placing them loftier than you ought to; you're instead seeing what a beautiful thing they offer this world and how lovely it is that they bring it to the table. If you view the details of yourself that are of that same caliber as worthy to be appreciated, you are not in a place of arrogance; rather, you are in a place of healthy love, esteem, and joy that you are putting out into the world something of golden value. Healthy self-esteem and the right confidence aren't thinking you are better than everyone else, but knowing that you hold a value and worthiness that goes beyond yourself, and it is needed in this world.

Developing confidence is not an all-or-nothing journey. It is a journey that takes time to love yourself and to feel comfortable in your own skin. It begins by choosing to allow yourself to grow in appreciation of who God made you to be, even if it's a slow progression. Confidence can also be developed in subtle ways. Perhaps you start a list of your traits that you would want to see your child adopt as part of their personality, approach toward life, etc. If you can appreciate it in your child, or hope for it in your future child, then perhaps you can begin to feel the same way toward yourself.

There was once a viral video where a mother shared that she hated her nose until her daughter was born, bearing her nose. Instead of looking at it as too large or not quite as straight as she would like, she realized what a beautiful part of this little girl it really was. The mom could appreciate in someone she loved something she hadn't appreciated in herself. We too can do the same, with or without a child of our own. Allow yourself the freedom to love in yourself what you love in others.

Know that a newly formed outlook on yourself and perhaps the world will have the potential to be distasteful to others. The phrase "you've changed" might be thrown around a bit, but aren't we supposed to change with time? Isn't the goal of a tree to grow and not remain a shrub? Others may have known you in your shrub era, but don't let that stop you from growing into the towering redwood you were always meant to be. You take away nothing from others by growing fully into yourself. In fact, those who are really for you will see all the splendor of the real you and find it not just tolerable but something to be celebrated.

Again, it is not a bad thing to love yourself. I am certainly not saying you ought to think you can do no wrong and that you are without reproach, but what I am saying is that you are someone worthy of love, including love that comes from you. What a gift it is to give the world the actual authentic and genuine sincere version of yourself instead of a fabricated reproduction of what you think the world wants. Real beauty comes from real people who know who they really are.

SEASONAL MISSION STATEMENT

Do you have a seasonal mission statement? Most people don't, but it may be an intriguing exercise in helping form your outlook and worldview as you make cognizant and intentional choices. A seasonal mission statement is not one requiring fanciful words, empowering imagery, or even action steps; rather it is a sturdy, secure anchor that you hold as you venture onward. I say "seasonal" because just as the seasons change, so do we, and we must be willing to alter or shift our focal points, missions, and goals with the times. Graham Cooke explains that there are three pieces of identity: your lens, how you think about it, and how you talk about it. A seasonal mission statement is a part of your identity moving forward.

This concept is rooted primarily in the idea that many of us choose at the beginning of each year to have a word, image, or phrase that serves as a theme for the year. That is a lofty goal set with good intentions, but the seasonal mission statement is a tad different. Instead of placing a direct timeline on the statement or goal, it is recognizing that our personal seasons very seldom adapt themselves to fit in with the calendar year, and it is less goal-oriented and more mindset purposed. It is the deliberate effort to live out one's purpose in due season with the grace that if it is not fully attained, it does not make one a failure.

This mission statement can change over time, just as missions change from season to season. For you practically, one mission statement could look like working on loving yourself more. It is a goal, but it is also more of a mindset shift to be kinder and more grace giving, and to speak life into your own self-concept rather than self-deprecation.

A dear friend of mine has done this, and she found that having an adjoining piece in the form of words can prove beneficial. For her it is often a verse from the Bible or a song lyric that really connects with her spirit. One option is to write the lyric or verse on a sticky note and place it on your mirror (I use a dry erase marker on my mirror) so that you cannot go a day without seeing it. You could even go as far as to take a sharpie and write the word, phrase, or a symbol of your mission statement on your arm. It can serve as a constant reminder that is not pushy, overbearing, unattainable, or heavy to carry. Instead, it is something that gives a smile as you navigate onward.

What could your mission statement be for the season you are currently in? Is there a specific aspect of your life or your self-concept that you would like to develop a more optimistic view of? Your attitude toward even difficult people or circumstances can shift when choose conscious ways to make the best of it. Invite God into the process—ask Him to give you a word, phrase, or metaphor for this current season of life, and ask how He wants to grow, mold, or teach you through the example He reveals to your heart.

A mission statement can also be geared toward a purpose statement. What is something that you bring to the table and this world that is needed, unique, and a gift to others and the world around you? The world needs you. Remind yourself of that through a purpose or mission statement and wear it on the days that you're prone to forget.

PERSONAL REFLECTION
AND APPLICATION QUESTIONS

1. In the level you are on now in life, what is one area you are finding difficult to master, overcome, or advance past?

2. Have you ever had a "sewing machine" story? What were you glad you had in your arsenal from a former lesson or season that came in handy?

3. Was there a friendship that you found to be seasonal but that massively impacted your life?

4. What is one aspect of who you really are that you can say you like and love about yourself?

CHAPTER 7

Flowering

*Trust in the LORD with all your heart
and lean not on your own understanding;
in all your ways submit to him,
and he will make your paths straight.*

—Proverbs 3:5,6

*It takes courage to grow up and
become who you really are.*

—E. E. Cummings

CURIOSITY OVER FEAR

"What if?" may perhaps be the most overused question an anxious mind can produce. With a mind that is wired with such a profound ability to think and imagine, what a pity it is when fear dominates, thwarts, and rips away all the joy that could be held. It steals away all the mystery that could be born in the most astonishing of ways if we instead approached situations with curiosity. What if we

115

rewired our brains to slide down the metaphorical rabbit hole marked with curiosity instead?

A curious mind is more concerned with the infinite number of adventures than the infinite ways something could end in calamity. A curious mind is also one that sees a problem as potential, for the story has not yet reached its end. A curious mind is more set with hope and the knowing that a problem is really an enigma, one that is yet to be fully revealed for the lesson or tale it holds.

There is a scene in the *Lord of the Rings: The Two Towers* where two of the sojourners on a quest have found themselves in a predicament that appears to be utterly and without a doubt hopeless. Instead of caving in to fear, instead of wearing a garment of dismay, one of the two approaches the conundrum with a sense of curiosity and hope about what could possibly await, for he believed in his spirit that they were not yet at the end. Sam shares,

I know. It's all wrong. By rights we shouldn't even be here. But we are. It's like in the great stories, Mr. Frodo. The ones that really mattered. Full of darkness and danger they were, and sometimes you didn't want to know the end. Because how could the end be happy? How could the world go back to the way it was when so much bad had happened? But in the end, it's only a passing thing, this shadow. Even darkness must pass. A new day will come. And when the sun shines it will shine out the clearer. Those were the stories that stayed with you... that meant something. Even if you were too small to understand why. But I think, Mr. Frodo, I do understand. I know now. Folk in those stories had lots of chances of turning back only they didn't. They kept going because they were holding on to something. Frodo: What are we holding on to, Sam? Sam: That there's some good in this world, Mr. Frodo. And it's worth fighting for.[8]

Sam knew that there was something of value worth continuing onward for, and that there was no way they had reached the end. He took on the spirit of curiosity in the way he knew that there was something beyond the shadows, and that there was yet something to be gained in the journey. It was something of good and of value to the world, and it was worthy of enduring onward for.

In the same way, when an event presents itself where we would at first instinctively react in fear, we too can take on the heart posture to instead approach with intrigue and intention to see it through. Second Timothy 1:7 also reminds us, "For God has not given us a spirit of fear and timidity, but of power, love, and self-discipline" (NLT). It is not the will of God that we live in fear, rather, that we live in hope rooted in God. When we look to Him and consider that He can do infinitely more than anything we can even imagine (Ephesians 3:20), we then can stand in a place of curiosity about how He will bring about a solution, not in a stature of fear that all hope is lost. Your worry will not solve the issue, nor will it help it at all. Instead of defaulting to the first option of fear, try considering what this might teach you that you could learn in no other way, and what an epic testimony this will one day be in the future. After all, who knows what could happen next?

FEARLESSLY AUTHENTIC

The mainstream isn't always toxic, but that doesn't mean you should drink from it as your only source. For those who are not of the Millennial generation, "mainstream" in this context is slang for commonplace practices. For many, the idea of breaking from how things have always been done, pivoting from what everyone else is doing, or making the choice to be a non-conformist is utterly terrifying, but what if? What if you walked to the drumbeat of your own heart's song? What would it mean for you personally to be fearless and authentic to your own wonderfully peculiar self?

You know what it would mean to live in a way that would be alternative to how most people do. To live in such a way that you were uninhibited by the confines of your mind and the limits you set on your life. You would no longer self-sabotage. You would no longer lessen yourself in order to make others feel more comfortable, and you would no longer live glancing over your shoulder to see if anyone is looking. When you stop living for the opinions of others and you start living for what brings you peace, it looks different, it feels different, and it has a different impact on the day-to-day that you live. Fireflies don't dim their lights to match the dark evening around them, they shine as they were designed to shine. Their light becomes a spectacle to us as onlookers, something of merriment and wonder. If a bug can unabashedly shine as it was created to, why can't you? Whether it produces a life where you are on the top of a mountain in the way of success or in your inner spirit, or both, you live in such a way as to have true freedom. You even enjoy being you.

The intricate details of how we are fashioned are pertinent reminders that we were made to be remarkably special. The fact that even identical twins have different fingerprints shows that, despite our similarities, there is woven within our very beings God's design for us to be unique. We are similar to snowflakes in that way, for with these crystalized drops of snow no two are ever alike. So, if such a thoughtful intention was placed upon frozen water, how much more was placed upon you? That being a salient fact of life, it then invites the question: How should I live in fulfillment of the intrinsic design that is me?

Only an intimate relationship with the One who fashioned you can really answer that. It is something that time reveals too, which you will spend a lifetime discovering. You'll find the more you come to know the Creator, the more you'll come to know yourself. The deeper you know the One who made you, the more it will come forward in time the reason you were made. That is not the reason you should seek Him, but it is a gift you'll come to open along the way in relationship. What a marvelous mystery it is, as you abide in God's Word, to allow Him to uncover all that is you and all that is not as He conforms you to His character. Also, the more you allow curiosity to be the flashlight you shine upon things, the more you will find what is you and what is not you. You are far from ordinary, even if you think you are typical, basic, and dispensable. Your life is a Cinderella slipper—it's one that can only and ever fit you.

In the course of living a fearlessly authentic life, you must also realize that it will not look like the lives of those around you. Sure, you are functioning as a human is designed to function—eating, sleeping, etc.—but you are living against the grain, in a different manner than the person next to you. It is the literal opposite of the cookie-cutter mentality. The singer Mama Cass put it this way: "You've gotta make your own music, sing your own special song, make your own kind of music even if nobody else sings along." There must be a willingness to sing solo, to live in a manner that is confident enough to stand as you really are, even if it is alone.

Although conceptually that does not sound preferable, it is wild how much abundance of peace is given in standing as you really are, the real you. Remember that in living out that truth you are ultimately reflecting Christ. Jesus reminds us, "No one lights a lamp and then puts it under a basket. Instead, a lamp is placed on a stand, where it gives light to everyone in the house. In the same way, let your good deeds shine out for all to see, so that everyone will praise your heavenly Father" (Matthew 5:15,16, NLT). Dimming your light or putting it under a shade not only hides the true you, but it dims His glory and that which He can do through you as vessel. Don't shade your light, for it shades His glory through you.

Choosing authenticity begins with a million small choices that one day will lead to every aspect of your life being fearlessly authentic. It is much like the winter breaking into spring. The sun shines down on the land and the snow begins to melt. The earth beckons that which is beneath the surface to become known and seen with brilliant color, and though it is seemingly slow every part embraces spring. It is not reserved only for certain areas, for spring demands fullness, even if it is timid in coming about. The same can be said in your life. The choice to make a minor adjustment that is true to the real you, the you that you were crafted to be, will over time invite more. Once you have tasted what it means to be you, two things begin to happen: first, you enjoy being you, and second, you will find all other options distasteful and counterfeit to what you know is real and right.

Taking upon yourself the heart to be fearlessly authentic also invokes the act of blooming right where you are. The entire concept of being a Wallflower That Bloomed is not that you have been moved to a different plot, that you were moved to the center of the room, or even that you stopped being a Wallflower. It means that you are fastidious in your pursuit of blooming right where you are, without the need for approval from mankind. You are unyielding to the peer pressures of society or the sideways glances from others, and you are at peace regardless of whether you are a spectacle to the world. You instead are no longer itchy in your own skin because it fits just right. That is not to say that you won't experience the need to test and try on what fits and what doesn't, much like Goldilocks, but once the true you is known, you will no longer feel the discomfort of the disingenuous self. There is no substitute for the real you. You are fulfilled because of who you are and who you belong to; there is no need for anything else. Fight for who you were always made to be and settle for nothing less, because who you were made to be, as a child of God, is worth fighting for.

BREAKING PEOPLE-PLEASING

It is human nature to crave affirmation, approval, and appreciation. These desires are not wrong, but as with anything in this life they can be twisted, and the result is the feeling of being used, taken advantage of, and ultimately burned out.

Often those of us with generous hearts, good manners, and a sincere desire to be helpful will find ourselves in the trap of people-pleasing. This trap is one in which we may not necessarily notice that we are being swayed into it, but the effects will certainly be felt. The feelings of burn-out and exhaustion can leave the heart worn, resentful, and without the option to say "no" to anyone. Despite these symptoms, many of us continue on the path of people-pleasing for years, even decades, but why is that? Perhaps some of us were raised that pleasing others is what is correct or how things are done. Some of us fear the rejection of others if we let them down by saying "no," or we fear their anger if we do not do as they ask. Some of us are also afraid of abandonment if we are no longer fulfilling a need, so we continue to help fearing we will be tossed aside if we are not continuously being used. Regardless of *why* we continue to people-please, the person who truly gets the short end of the stick is you. You are worth so much more than being constantly used by those around you.

As followers of Christ, we are called to live as Christ did, including serving others. Jesus tells us, "If I then, the Lord and the Teacher, washed your feet, you also ought to wash one another's feet. For I gave you an example that you also should do as I did to you" (John 13:14,15, NASB95). The key is that we connect with God to ensure that we are obediently following what He desires us to do rather than taking someone's role.

Part of partaking in our daily bread is recognizing what we need daily to be sustained by God, but it is also acknowledging that we are given an assignment from God in how to live out the day He has graciously given. Consider it like the manna that was given by God to the people of Israel while traveling in the desert. God sent manna, similar to wafered bread, to fall from heaven six days a week to sustain the people. Their daily tasks required sustenance, and God gave them the exact portion they needed. For us today, we can look for manna in what He gives by His Spirit for sustenance and by what we are called to do for Him. Some days that may include helping others, and some days that may include just caring for yourself.

Colossians 3:23 tells us, "Work willingly at whatever you do, as though you were working for the Lord rather than for people" (NLT). When we are called to serve others, we ought to do it with the heart posture that it is for the glory of God and in obedience to what He has given us to do, not for the approval of man. This is why doing heart check-ins are so important, because when we sit honestly before the Lord with our open heart, we will then see if we are helping others because He has called us to do so or if there is the hidden idol of people's approval moving us to serve. A good friend of mine once conveyed it in this way: "If we are people-pleasing, we are not God-pleasing, so that is why it is important to check our hearts for motive." After we have checked our hearts and surrendered to the Lord to obey His call, we can then live with healthy boundaries so that all are cared for as He desires.

Boundaries can feel uncomfortable when we put them in place, but ultimately, they are for the benefit of all who are impacted. This can look different depending on the circumstances, but it can start with asking God where our focus ought to be in that season. Perhaps someone you have helped in the past is not for this season and God is calling you to step down to make room for someone else to serve, and there is nothing wrong with that. In fact, God may be asking you to leave a seat because He has someone's call and destiny awaiting them in the seat you are currently occupying.

Another aspect of setting healthy boundaries is using good communication. This can look like using kind words but not weak ones. Let your "no" be no and your "yes" be yes without waffling or wavering. Lastly, setting a healthy boundary requires your reliance to be on God so that even if someone becomes upset or angered by your answer, your self-perception, self-worth, and self-esteem are not dependent on others but on God alone. Healthy boundaries benefit everyone, though it may take time for others to realize such truths.

The road to recovering from being a people-pleaser is not always easy, but it will prove correct in the end. Ultimately when you follow God and serve Him as He asks, not serve those around you who are asking you, it is then that you will see fruit in your life that is produced by the Spirit. You will also find that even in seasons where you are doing much, God will provide the ability and strength to keep going. When we are God-pleasing and not people-pleasing, it is then that we are living in a healthy way—a way that is honoring God and fulfilling our destiny here on earth.

VICTIMHOOD ISN'T YOUR IDENTITY

It is imperative that we find the correct manner of validating what we endured in the past, but also that we do not fall into the trap of making victimhood our identity. Your experience, be it fifteen years ago or fifteen minutes ago, of a time when your heart was bruised, your soul was wounded, or your self-esteem shaken does deserve to be recognized. After you have properly processed the event, you rise up and move on so that it does not continue to thwart you by making you out to be a victim.

Pinpointing the root event that caused lasting effects can help you understand aspects of your current status. Bullying unfortunately does not stop in the schoolyard or lunchroom, even as adults it is not uncommon, but you hold the power to choose whether to have a victim mindset or not. Do not allow being the "bullied one" or having a sad tale to become your identity— not just in how you see yourself but in how you present yourself to others. You are so much more than that, and it is about time the world and you get to see the person behind the trauma.

This is presented well in *The Princess Diaries.* Mia, the main character, is a fifteen-year-old who is constantly bullied for just about everything and anything, from her looks to her ability to present a speech in class. Her life drastically changes when she learns she is the royal heir to the throne of Genovia, and with that fact comes a makeover for her hair, wardrobe, and beyond. Her fellow students then find her new look to be trying too hard, and they mock her even more. Once the secret is out about her identity, she suddenly becomes the person everyone wants to befriend, but she makes a powerful move that we can all learn from. Instead of manipulating others with her newfound popularity and instead of playing the victim card, she blooms. She stands unashamed and unyielding to her true self, fully acknowledging she is a work in progress. What is essential for us to adopt from Mia's journey is that our identities are not entwined with being victims or victors; our identities are the awareness that we are all works in progress working through all that has been and all that is, toward all we hope to be in the future. Identity is the collection of myriad petals blooming in their own time.

We must watch ourselves that we avoid a victim mentality. When life has handed you some rotten eggs, it is easy to continuously agree with the idea that you are unlucky, forgotten, or stuck. It is one thing to wallow for an afternoon, but it is completely different to add those beliefs to the invisible name tag you wear on your chest to tell the world how to identify you. Stop agreeing to lies, conspiracies, and myths made up by your anxiety and the self-pity monster that resides within. The story isn't over yet, so don't assume you know the ending. Even if others say these things about you, don't join in that chorus. A well-meaning friend once semi-jokingly said, "Nothing good ever happens to Cally," and I would be lying if I said those words haunted me, but the choice to agree with him rests in my own hands. At the time life was in a hurricane-level storm, but I knew that wasn't my lot in life. That season did not last forever, and although life is not by any means ideal all the time, I have the choice even now years later to agree with Stan or not that nothing good happens to me. It's easy to be a victim, but you choose the tag associated with your role in your own story. Will you be the victim, or will you be the protagonist of your own story? Only you can make that decision, but remember winners are never self-affirmed victims.

Scars remind us of things that have occurred in our past. The scars may be within, or the scars may be worn like tattoos you never consented to obtain; either way, they serve as reminders of what once was and what we had to endure. Yet scars are not the whole of the person, and that is paramount in how we view them. You are more than your scars, even if they are sizable. Consider how much of yourself you keep from being shared and known and revealed if you are fixated on the one scar. That is what a victim mentality does: it impairs us from seeing beyond the suffering, beyond the trauma, and beyond the past. There are so many more elements of your personality, skills, talents, and all you bring to the table than just your hurts. In being more than a victim, make what is known of you more than just the scars.

You and you alone can choose what the narrative is—whether you are a victim or someone who has seen heartache—but that is only part of the story. Don't cheat yourself and others out of knowing the whole of you in focusing only on a single piece, because that's the real sad tale. The saddest tale of all is you and others missing out on the treasure of all of you by only bringing up the unfortunate parts. Don't miss the forest for the trees.

PERSONAL REFLECTION
AND APPLICATION QUESTIONS

1. What is one issue in your life right now that you can approach with curiosity over fear?

2. Who is the fearlessly authentic version of you really? How do you live this out and what does it look like in action?

3. If people-pleasing is something you struggle with, what is your first step toward healthy boundaries and better communication so that you are not left feeling displeased and used?

4. In what practical ways can we shift away from allowing past hurts to become the focus of our identities?

CHAPTER 8

The Blooming

Live the full life of the mind, exhilarated by new ideas,
intoxicated by the romance of the usual.

—**Ernest Hemingway**

For you created my inmost being;
you knit me together in my mother's womb.
I praise you because I am fearfully and wonderfully
made; your works are wonderful, I know that full well.

—**Psalm 139:13,14**

USING WHAT YOU'VE GOT IN
YOUR KNAPSACK

You have been equipped with a custom-tailored set of abilities. Over the course of your life, many of these are impacted, either by growth or dampening, and others are acquired along the way. Let's take a look at what you are currently equipped with, and how you can utilize those tools in your own personal knapsack to the fullest potential.

EMPATHY

Empathy is the ability to discern, imagine, or share in what it would be like to be in another person's shoes for an experience. Some seem to be born with a substantial ability for empathy simply because it is woven into the fabric of their being. For others, empathy is cultivated from a root of trauma, meaning they grow in empathy because they have experienced trauma during their own lives and are therefore able to then offer empathy toward others. This is a case of taking something meant for harm in your life and pivoting to its use being for good going forward. Empaths are typically deep feelers. They can sometimes become overwhelmed if they take on the feelings of another person as if the event were happening directly to them. God bless these souls. The level of empathy one can feel is hard to measure and is completely dependent on the situation at hand.

Empathy is much like the various amounts of crayons you can purchase in a box set. For some, empathy is the simple primary colors package; it is closer to the realm of sympathy, which is feeling emotion for someone's situation rather than feeling the emotion with them. Others have been given the mega sixty-four Crayola pack of empathy. They can discern and express the exact sentiments felt with a situation, even if they themselves have never experienced that exact situation. The full spectrum of emotions and colors are understood because of this substantial sixty-four pack they possess. Those of us with the sixty-four packs can often burden ourselves with the overwhelm of taking on some very heavy situations. This is where those with the mega pack need to utilize the additional add-on included with the sixty-four pack—the sharpener in the back. Use that tool to sharpen your awareness of what is really your responsibility to take on with the other person and what does not require your full involvement. No one uses the sharpener quite right the first time, but discernment is a muscle grown over time as it's exercised, not something instantly spurred overnight. Empathy is a great superpower, but you must use it in such a way that it does not overwhelm or drain you.

SYMPATHY AND APPROACH

Sympathy is commiserating with someone's feelings, and is something helpful you can tap into. Many times, people do not need us to feel what they're feeling, they simply need someone to listen and offer kindness. This is when pulling out the sympathy crayon is useful, and it will prove the healthiest route for all parties included. A useful practice that I've learned along the way, to know exactly what the other person needs without me assuming, is to ask them a series of questions: What do you need? Do you need me to just listen, to help fix the issue, to round up ideas with you, or to leave you to just handle it on your own? Do you need me, or do you need space?

Depending on the situation, I will also offer a facetious idea to invoke a chuckle or at minimum a slight grin. It can help lighten the mood when someone really needs it. Asking the series of questions also allows you to know how much the other person desires for you to be involved in the situation and it establishes healthier boundaries in your relationship. This is not to negate when someone is in serious danger and more action must be taken, but you are wise enough to know when those situations are at hand and how to respond. Offering a sympathetic ear or hand can be useful and a gift depending on the situation, but this is also where using good discernment and reading the room is imperative.

IMAGINATION

Imagination is perhaps the most fascinating and wondrous of the resources in your metaphorical knapsack. It is in a way the snow globe in your knapsack: when you shake it, the scene that emerges after the swirling snow dissipates is one of truly any possibility. If empathy is the sixty-four pack of Crayolas, imagination is the span of the entire Milky Way. Consider how every book in the world, including the one you are reading in this very moment, is the result of someone's God-given imagination. But how can you help your imagination flourish, and what is the best way to utilize such a gift?

For some, you may have found there was a time in life where imagination was frightening. It may have felt, or currently feel, like a hot-air balloon that was majestic to look at, outrageously fun to ride in, but that had very little user control that wouldn't result in disaster. In truth, fear was dominating in greater power. Fear will leech off imagination in the form of worry, but worry is a poor use of imagination. Worry is the collection of "what ifs" and disastrous conclusions based off conspiracy theories of your own life. I do not believe that was the original intent of imagination, and it thwarts all the beauty of wonderful possibilities to come. It invites a dark raincloud on a cloudless day of 75 degrees. Anxiety is a real monster in the closet to fight off, but it is not one that must have the final word, and it does not have to become the parasite that sucks the life blood out of your imagination.

If you are one who knows you have a very vivid imagination but keep it at bay with a strongly roped tether, I will remind you softly but ardently not to confuse perspective with reality. We often assume that things are one certain way but it really is perspective that offers a fuller view. You can imagine a faux Ficus is real and water it all you want, but it's never going to actually grow. You perceived it to be real, but it was truthfully made of plastic. Don't confuse delusion with perspective, because if you do there is the great possibility of missing out on astronomical levels of creativity, invention, and discovery.

Imagination is the wellspring of some of the greatest pieces of art, music, architecture, and beauty this world holds. It all began with a dream and idea in someone's mind, and to keep that creativity gated from the world affects not only you but everyone around you. Loosen that tether a bit and see where imagination will take you. You might just find the world to be a little brighter, and discover that possibilities being endless is not a bad thing. Above all else dare to dream, because it really is the color added to an otherwise bland, clockwork world. You were given an imagination for a reason, so don't squander it in the name of practicality and reason.

NEURODIVERGENT AND
NEUROTYPICAL TENDENCIES

Recent years have produced a spike in interest regarding brain function and study, and consequently research has increased our understanding of how the brain works. This book is not meant to be a science textbook or a collection of research studies, but I would be remiss if I did not touch on understanding oneself in the way of neuro-processing and function as well.

Someone who is "neurotypical" has a brain that functions in the typical way, which is the norm for most people. Neurodivergent persons, on the other hand, make up less of the population, and their brains function in a different way. One is not better than or less than the other, it is more of a reality that you are either one or the other. For those who fall in the category of neurodivergent, you may find the gift of self-acceptance greater when you understand that your brain does not operate like the majority of people, and there is absolutely nothing wrong with you because of that. Your brain is not broken. When you understand more of how your brain is wired, you may stop hating on yourself as much.

For me personally it took several years before a proper diagnosis came about with my neurodivergence. That isn't rare for girls especially, as we are not tested as much as boys, and typically we do a better job of masking. My journey to diagnosis came in parts. I had a friend who is on the autism spectrum recognize habits and quirks of mine that were in alignment with neurodivergence, and he was curious if I was in that camp of the population. I blew it off for years, but with the rise of others sharing about their own sensory issues, habits, and ways their brains worked I began to question if he was correct. Long story short, I was tested, and it did confirm that I am certainly neurodivergent. To me it came not as a surprise but as a gift. For all the things I used to condemn myself for doing, the ways I was not like everyone else, the ways I considered myself not normal, I began to give myself grace for. I stopped asking an electric car to run on gasoline.

Below are some of the categories that fall under the greater umbrella of neurodiversity, and I would advise anyone who thinks there is a chance they may have an electric car brain to follow up with a professional for testing and answers. It can also help you learn techniques on how to work with how your brain operates, not against it. The world is not designed for neurodivergence, but there is a way to make your corner of the world more comfortable, agreeable, and functional so that you can thrive in your environment and the world around you. Knowledge of how your brain is wired will make it more accessible for you to excel in life. An article in *Forbes* gives more explanation:

Neurodivergent individuals often experience differences in mental function, learning styles, sensory processing, communication styles and behaviors. They may struggle with soft skills such as emotional intelligence, social interactions or the ability to work effectively in a group. Other physical behaviors —such as standing too close to someone, speaking too loudly or self-soothing actions like rocking or irregular hand movement—may also be present.

Below are some mental health conditions that fall in the neurodivergent category, according to Pankhuree Vandana, M.D., a pediatric psychiatrist and medical director at the Center for Autism Spectrum Disorder at Nationwide Children's Hospital in Columbus, Ohio.

- **ADHD.** Individuals may have difficulties holding their attention and managing thoughts, behaviors and emotions.

- **Autism.** Also called spectrum disorder, this includes a broad range of conditions that may include challenges with socializing and social skills, cause repetitive behaviors and trigger speech difficulties, which in some cases, may lead an individual to communicate only nonverbally.

- **Dyslexia.** This can include misreading, miswriting or misspeaking certain items, as well as confusion with letters or misunderstanding of word organization or pronunciation, and trouble following directions.

- **Dyscalculia.** A misunderstanding of math concepts, such as confusion when reading numbers and symbols, an inability to consistently remember numbers, math facts, rules and procedures, or trouble with mental figuring.

- **Dysgraphia.** A learning disability that involves writing, such as unusual pencil grip and body position, illegible handwriting and an aversion to writing or drawing.[9]

For those reading this who do not find connection to the signs of neurodiversion, I would suggest still doing some research. It can prove a wonderful tool to have a greater understanding of those around you who might be navigating learning how to use their brain in a world that was not designed for how their brain functions best. Also, by recognizing that we all bring to the table something of inherent value with our differences, it will help you grow as a person in loving others well.

Neurotypical or neurodivergent, we all bring something of value to the way our world works. When we can work together to celebrate these differences and to help those who are struggling find that sweet spot of acceptance and allowance to thrive, it is only then that we see where all the gears work well together.

GIFTS OF THE SPIRIT

What is your spiritual gift? Romans 12 gives a list, so let's see where you fall. Some people may have been given more than one:

For just as each of us has one body with many members, and these members do not all have the same function, so in Christ we, though many, form one body, and each member belongs to all the others. We have different gifts, according to the grace given to each of us. If your gift is prophesying, then prophesy in accordance with your faith; if it is serving, then serve; if it is teaching, then teach; if it is to encourage, then give encouragement; if it is giving, then give generously; if it is to lead, do it diligently; if it is to show mercy, do it cheerfully. (Romans 12:4–8)

Romans compares those in Christ to the human body. Each part serves a purpose, and each purpose is important. When these gifts are placed together within a community, there is an abundance of growth that can exponentially occur. When two or more are gathered, He is there (Matthew 18:20). When two or more work together, imagine the success that can come forth.

PROPHECY

The gift of prophecy is one often highly ignored in the church. Typically, modern church status quo is to shut up the word given by the Spirit. It is sometimes thought to be fake, just a scheme to make money or earn fame, but what does God say about prophecy? First Thessalonians 5:19–22 says, "Do not quench the Spirit. Do not treat prophecies with contempt but test them all; hold on to what is good, reject every kind of evil." Do not extinguish the Spirit, for God's Holy Spirit should not be someone we reject or ignore. Rather, embrace the Spirit. Ask the Lord to come and vividly speak to you. John 10 speaks of how good it is when the sheep know the Shepherd's voice, so why would we reject God speaking to us? Often, it is through a dream, a vision, or a 3 a.m. wakeup call. Whether it is an audible voice or a deeply rooted feeling, we must not reject the voice of God in our lives. The most vital piece of this verse beyond not quenching the Spirit is that we must test all things. First John 4:1 speaks of testing the spirits, meaning we must fully ensure the message is of God and not of man. To do so, we must bring forth the proper balance of Scripture and Spirit in our lives so that we in turn have proper balance within our own lives. In doing this, we do not fall into legalism or an overly spiritual place where the enemy can grab us, but rather we are within the will of God and within His borders.

So how do we get to a firm understanding? First, we pray. We pray for confirmation in Scripture. I like to ask for three confirmations from God on big things. Typically, first, I ask for a Bible verse to confirm, since the voice of God will never contradict the Word of God (Numbers 23:19). This is a direct communication. Next, I ask for confirmation through a fellow believer, such as through discussion within a community of believers who sincerely seek to embrace what God has for His children, or for an overwhelming peace that can only come from Him. This is an indirect communication. Lastly, I ask for a third-party confirmation. This could be a vanity plate, a sign from somewhere, or a complete "coincidence" that gives a confirmation. Regardless of the conduit, the peace of knowing that only God can give such a confirmation is often overwhelming. This is an outside source communication, but it allows for a balance within the spectrum of a well-rounded confirmation.

Do not reject what the Spirit may be doing, if He's prompting you to speak to someone, because you may just encourage that person or even save a life. To quench the Spirit would be to allow fear to tune out those nudges and ignore His voice. Think of a peaceful spring day with the sounds of birds singing. An array of songbirds graces the air with subtle yet peaceful songs, but then comes a squawking crow. We are the ones to choose which sound to tune into. The harmonious, placid voice of truth, or the fretful discord of an intruder. Both voices are present, but it is the one you choose to give attention to that will impact your actions.

One night I was awakened from a deep sleep at 3 a.m. with the overwhelming feeling to pray for a friend. I felt God saying to pray for my friend Jamie, and that she was aching that she could not have a child. I had not spoken to Jamie in over a year, so she was most definitely not at the forefront of my subconscious. I did not question, rather, I prayed. I interceded for her and her husband to have a child. I did not tell her about it, but two days later she shared on social media how happy she was for those around her having kids, but that she ached not to have a child of her own. What a truly humbling experience it was for me to call her and tell her that God Himself had awakened me to pray for her regarding that exact weight on her heart. God heard her heart, and He wanted to express that to her so vividly that He used another believer to tell her so. I am tearing up now thinking about it, for I am so humbled that He used me in such a way. I say all of this to encourage you, my friend, to not reject the voice of God. If we want to hear from God, we must be willing to listen.

TEACHING

You do not have to know math, English, or a foreign language to teach. A teacher is someone who shares and instructs someone else with the knowledge they have. It is like sharing with someone how to make bread so that they will not starve. Are you a teacher?

In teaching, the best thing to remember is that the Holy Spirit is the One doing the work. You are there to show up and be obedient, but you do not have to have all the answers. Whether the teaching involves children or adults, taking the time to share with someone else can impact a life greatly. This can also be called mentorship. We are called to pour into those younger than us, or those around us who need instruction. There is no age limit regarding how you can pour into someone. Mentorship is so important in today's technological society, for the human element has become a true rarity in a world built around technology, but that makes its necessity even more vital. We must not allow technology to steal the true essence of what our hearts are made for. It says in Genesis 2:18 that it is not good for man to be alone, and as such we need each other. We need each other to grow—to learn from, to teach, and to help.

Mentoring is a beautiful ministry that embraces this, but also changes us in the process. Throughout the Scriptures we see examples of mentorship, from Elijah mentoring Elisha to Jesus mentoring the disciples." Teachers embrace the call of good discernment, devoted study of Scripture and human behavior, and patience. Discernment comes from a vibrant and dedicated relationship with God. Coming into a deeper relationship with God will enable the teacher to share godly wisdom with others. Allowing the Holy Spirit to work through the teacher blesses the teacher to assist and mentor those seeking guidance. Devoted study in the Word of God is the beginning of such wisdom. Knowing the Scriptures only adds to the knowledge of God Himself. Consider it the most important manual and textbook a teacher—or anyone—can own. Finally, patience is key. Patience is truly listening and hearing those around you, listening and hearing God, and listening and hearing the wisdom of those who have gone before you. Patience is a virtue, and certainly a necessity for a teacher. Embrace being a teacher and you may be surprised at how God will use you.

ENCOURAGEMENT

Do you have the gift of encouraging others? When you see someone who is down or depressed, are you there with a kind word to lift them up? Proverbs 16:24 wisely conveys that "Kind words are like honey—sweet to the soul and healthy for the body" (NLT). Perhaps God has you in a particular person's life on a particular day for a reason. Pray for wisdom about how to encourage them. Lift them up with a word, prayer, or an act of kindness. Encouragement can be as small as a smile. You never know how you may change a life by simply being kind. Time commitment is a vital piece of encouragement. Not in devoting oneself to the point of exhaustion, but in being the kind of person who will be present and willing to help even at 3 a.m. Much of the earthly ministry of Christ Himself was spent selflessly encouraging those around Him. Jesus got on their level; He did not walk arrogantly over to the tax collectors and prostitutes with a condemning arrogance. Rather, He got on their level. He loved them, and perhaps that is the greatest healing that we can participate in: to help someone feel loved and seen.

GIVING

Have you been blessed with money? Money—in any amount—is a blessing to be shared. When the rich young leader came to Jesus, Jesus instructed him to share his wealth and follow Him. The young ruler left saddened at this, but he forfeited the greatest wealth in the world that day in exchange for earthly riches. Do not store up riches here on earth, for moth, rust, and time can destroy. Rather, store up riches in heaven and share with others. If God has given you earthly goods, share them. Malachi 3:10 promises that God will give you back even more, so you have nothing to lose. Money is not meant to be hoarded, but it is meant to be shared and to help those in need.

Giving does not require a six-figure salary. It is vital to remember the poor widow who gave her last two coins in Mark 12. She had only two coins and still gave them in sacrifice. Romans 12:1 calls us to live as living sacrifices to the Lord; this means giving of ourselves to others for the Lord and going that extra mile. Giving can sometimes look like simply taking the time to listen. People do not just need us to spend a few dollars to help them. Sometimes, they need us to spend time on them. They need our concern and compassion. To give is to receive the blessing of helping another person God created.

LEADING

Are you a leader? Do you feel called to lead a small group, a team, or even a church? Do you feel led to lead a team at work? Do not merely gloss over this and move on but ponder and pray to see if God is calling you to lead in a certain area. It is God who raises up leaders, so perhaps He is calling you. If that is the case, how can you become a better leader? Where can the wisdom to do so be found? Proverbs is a book of wisdom and guidance in being a good leader. Dive into Proverbs and look to others who exhibit good traits of leadership.

Leaders do not take a back seat when they feel called. They rise to the occasion and seek to foster order and stability for a communal effort. Pastors are often leaders, but anyone can be a leader. Perhaps you could organize and lead a small group or a Bible study to help others embrace community and reflection on Scripture. Spiritual gifts come in different forms; one is not greater than another in use. Just as a hand does not serve the same function as a foot, one gift can assist in the work of the Kingdom drastically different from another. Discern through prayer what gifts you possess, and then use them. Don't waste the literal talents the Father has lavished upon you. When you embrace and utilize the gifts His Spirit has placed within you, then even more dynamic aspects of your identity will be realized. Using such gifts vibrantly adds to a fuller understanding of your identity, for you come to know more of who you were made to be.

FINDING YOUR PEOPLE AND LIVING OUT YOUR PASSIONS PRACTICALLY

As mentioned before, when you are a Wallflower, it can often feel excessively difficult to find "your people." Even among the outsiders, we don't all seem to fit together as a collected group, but that doesn't mean you won't find your people eventually. You just need to know how to locate them. It can also be hard to know where to start to cultivate a life in which you live out your passions fully, but all these things can come together slowly.

Much of finding your people spurs from cultivating a life that attracts like minds and like hearts. It is more than just joining a club or social group; it's fostering the environment in which you grow too. When a tree is planted in a pot, it will only grow to the level that the roots have room to sink in properly in the soil. It won't reach its full potential because it does not have the space to do so. The same can be said of people. If they are confined in a pot metaphorically speaking, the potential wired within to reach their highest capacity is likewise confined. This could look like the job you are currently in. Does it absolutely thwart any ability you have to extend yourself creatively? Does it snuff out the spark that could flare up into a bonfire of so much more? I'm not telling you to quit your job on the spot, but I am challenging you to take a purposeful look at your current career or job and ask yourself whether it is helpful or harmful to you as a person. Are you chasing your passion, or are you just chasing a payday? Is the limited time you have on this planet worth that? How much value do you place on the years that you have been given on this earth? It is important for us as humans to question the environments we have found ourselves in from time to time because you might be a redwood stuck in a corner cubicle.

There is also the realization that you at some point will not meet the expectations others set on you. These may be expectations placed on you by a parent, by a romantic partner, by a friend, or by yourself. This is where we must swallow the pill of truth that we cannot please everyone or meet their expectations all the time. It is ironic how programs made for children can showcase this in a way that the adults watching can find encouragement as well. When I was a kid, every year during the holidays the Christmas special *Rudolph the Red-Nosed Reindeer* would air at least once. If it has been a while since you've seen the classic, the short film is about a reindeer, Rudolph, who is mocked and teased because his nose is a bright, shimmering red, atypical of the rest of the deer. Rudolph finds friendship with an elf, Hermey, who relates to Rudolph. Rudolph's father, Donner, sought to place mud on his son's nose to make him like the rest with the expectation of him fitting in, and Hermey empathizes in that there is the expectation for him to become a tinker-toy maker but he really desires to become a dentist.

The pair ventures on a journey and finds haven on the Island of Misfit Toys, where the inhabitants are exiled outcasts. There was nothing internally wrong with the toys, they were not hateful creatures, but their quirky exteriors made them unlike the rest. At the end of the story, all the citizens of the island are matched perfectly with children who need them and identify with them, for the recipients of the toys were in a way "misfits" as well. The moral of the story is that our differences make us who we are, and that is not a bad thing. The irony of the island is that though the toys were labeled "misfits" by some, by others they were just right, well received, and admired for their differences. In our own lives, even as adults, we too can adopt the attitude that being labeled a misfit by some isn't the case for all. For some you may be just right, and who knows, you may even save the day like Rudolph did.

In a more biblically sourced example of this, we see some of the artistic liberties that have been taken in portraying the apostle Matthew in *The Chosen*. In the series, which chronicles the ministry of Christ on earth, Jesus calls Matthew, an accomplished tax collector. Matthew is chosen by Christ to follow Him, but he finds it difficult to fit in with some of the other followers. Much of this is due to his former profession as a tax collector, where he was considered a traitor to the Jewish people in siding with Rome. In the series, there are also hints that Matthew may possibly be on the autism spectrum, and with that social interactions are navigated differently on his part in contrast to his peers. What is beautiful in this portrayal of Matthew is how Jesus accepts and loves him. Because of how Matthew is loved by Christ, the other disciples begin to accept him the more they seek to be like Christ, and the affection is sincere. Finding our people can take time, and it may take Christ revealing to them your value and worth.

When you have some of these internal heart aspects more reflective of your true self, then you will find the trend tends to trickle out into other aspects of your life. As you are watering the roots, the rest of the surrounding area tends to receive nourishment as well. Consider your social life. Do the friends around you make you feel included? Are you in a group of people you are glad to have as your social circle? We talked about this more in depth previously, but it's good to consider again. Remember that it's more about quality over quantity. When you are living in such a way that your internal life is reflected in and through you, the right people will notice and be magnetized toward you.

One aspect of inviting the right people into your life is to place yourself in the right gardens. If you really love hiking, are you out there doing it, or are you just talking about loving it? If you feel inclined to paint, are you actively taking classes for it, or are you just daydreaming about it? You may find that when you engage in activities that mean something to you, you will meet new groups of people whom you share those interests with. It is possible to be a dreamer and a doer, but it's on you if you live that out.

Lastly, cultivating a life of passion and inviting others into it requires you to let people in. Many Wallflowers find it fearsome to let someone into our own little worlds. In *Good Will Hunting*, Robin Williams's character said, "We get to choose who we let into our weird little worlds." He was right; it's up to us who we want to let in, but what a joy it is to let someone into our own little pillow fort of a world. How much more fun is it to let another person in to enjoy it with, not just doing it solo. They don't have to be in every aspect of your life to be a part of your world too, but consider taking the risk to let someone in. The right people will find you and you will find them, and it'll come just in the right timing as it should. Don't lose heart; a friend is on the way.

YOUR HAVEN

Beyond your profession as an aspect of your environment, we must also look at the space where we are abiding. Does your home reflect your heart? Big budgets are not necessary to do this. For example, for a long time I felt like I needed to model my room after an Ikea showroom or a snapshot from *HGTV*, but one day I realized that wasn't giving me peace. It was me attempting to replicate someone else's concept of peace.

So, I took action and let my room reflect my heart, not someone else's heart. This looked like taking cedar tree rounds from my friend's yard (he recently had a tree fall) and I added brackets to the bottom, some shellac to preserve the bark, and a few other inexpensive yet creative adjustments to make myself tree-round shelves. I collected wildflowers from a nearby field and preserved them with hairspray and bunched them with twine and hung them up on the wall, and I made my room literally a nest for myself. I also hung up a print from an Etsy shop that looked like a fine art portrait of a Taco Bell meal. It's earthy and quirky just like me, but I will tell you I have so much more peace than I did with my room looking like a knock-off budget version of the Target home section. My surrounding space didn't need to be aesthetically pleasing to anyone else but me, because after all it is me living in the space on a day-to-day basis. We can often be impacted emotionally by our environments, so make your home environment one in which you thrive.

Investing in hobbies can prove a bigger component of your environment than you may realize as well. Hobbies are often seen as a luxury, as we spend our time doing them knowing they more than likely will not yield money, just dopamine. For many of us, surrendering time in that manner is a luxury, but are you not worth that? Are you not worthy of even twenty minutes executing something you really, truly enjoy doing just for you? Hobbies are also great ways for you to navigate possibilities of adding to that metaphorical knapsack of what makes you, you. At time, hobbies can sneak up on you and reveal themselves to be something more than a hobby. Don't enter the hobby with the hope to find a profession along the way, but instead allow yourself to try something you have not done yet to see if it is really tailored for you. Remember that you don't need to be good at your hobby for it to be worthwhile. When ice skating you can spend a great majority of the time slipping straight down to the ground, and it may still be something you love and enjoy. A hobby is a gift you give to your true self to cultivate more of a life in which you actually live, not just meagerly exist.

Professions, housing, and hobbies are all macro ways to live out your passions, but there are micro ways to stir this up as well. If music is important to you, make it a point to have your life surrounded by music. Not just on the car radio, but get a little Bluetooth speaker for your kitchen to play some of your favorites while you make your morning coffee. Set aside fifteen minutes in the afternoon for tea by yourself to read, to ponder and contemplate life, to pray, or to just enjoy something that refreshes your soul. Giant moves are not necessary to cultivate a blooming life; little shifts can do this too. If movies are something that really get you going, set aside one evening a week where you have your own personal movie night. An old classic, a personal favorite, or something new to add to the things that you really find make life abundant. Micro shifts add up to the bigger macro that is your life.

Cultivating a haven for yourself and a true home, not just a living space, will make an astronomical different in whether you can find peace. Even subtle habits and remodels can make a big difference, from your home to your hobbies.

HELPING OTHERS BLOOM

There is something quite marvelous about how a candle works. A lit candle has the capacity to light another candle without dimming its own light, for the flame continues; yet it has shared what it retains of light, warmth, and substance. In the same way, once you experience the gift of blooming into who God truly made you to be, you can help light the candle of another.

Recall our ongoing analogy of the lunch table and what a difference it would have made, or did make, in your own life to be included, to be wanted, to be invited to come and sit. You can now do that for someone else. It does not matter how old you are or the profession you are in; that metaphorical lunch table covers myriad facets in connecting socially and emotionally. Encouraging and lifting someone up is one of the greatest ways you can share positivity and light in a world desperate for it.

Offering your authentic and non-judgmental self is a gift to those around you. Not a single one of us is in a place to cast the first stone, but we can still offer kindness, love, and a listening ear to those around us. We can offer encouragement and a lending hand, and we can offer someone else that flame of life in Christ, which will never go out, by lovingly sharing the gospel of everlasting life with them. Offering such things will not dim your light, but it will help fill the room with more light.

Use wisdom and discernment to act wisely, but if you feel a nudge that won't seem to let up, it may be part of your story to bless another's tale. You have no idea the impact you could have on another life.

PERSONAL REFLECTION
AND APPLICATION QUESTIONS

1. What resources are available in your knapsack in the way of empathy or sympathy?

2. Have you ever stifled or limited your imagination out of fear? When was that, and if you had chosen not to, how do you think the story could have been different?

3. What aspects of your home would you like to change to make it your peaceful place, rather than someone else's vision of a peaceful space?

4. What spiritual gift(s) do you possess?

5. Do you readily let people into your "weird little world," or are you more reluctant due to fear or trauma responses? What would be necessary in order for you to open the door to the pillow fort?

6. What ideas do you have of how to cultivate a life you love?

CHAPTER 9

The Gardener

We have come from God, and inevitably the myths woven by us, though they contain error, will also reflect a splintered fragment of the true light, the eternal truth that is with God. Indeed only by myth-making, only by becoming "sub-creator" and inventing stories, can Man aspire to the state of perfection that he knew before the Fall.

—J. R. R. Tolkien

However, you are not in the flesh but in the Spirit, if indeed the Spirit of God dwells in you.
—Romans 8:9 (NASB95)

THE GREAT GARDENER

Through the course of this book, we have looked at what it means to bloom and what it means to step into all that you were destined and created to be; but ultimately, we need to look first and foremost at the Great Gardener. To understand fully and properly who we are and why we were created, we must look to the One who made us in the first place. Because what is the art without the Artist, and what is the creation without the Creator? We cannot go on thinking every answer can be gleaned without looking at the One who destined it all to be.

God is the Gardener of the beautifully wonderful wildflower that is you. You are not just the leftovers of some primordial soup; you have so much more meaning, depth, and purpose than some theory of goo. You were woven and crafted with a very specific purpose in mind. That can be hard for some of us to allow ourselves to believe when we struggle with self-doubts and insecurities, but those doubts and insecurities are not what define us. We have meaning because of who made us. We have value because we were made in His image and placed in the world to add value by our existence. Yes, evil people and events are in the world, but even in a fallen creation we have a Father in heaven who wants to know us, help us, walk with us in hard times, and above all else love us.

The original heart of God for man was relationship in a garden. This is vibrantly showcased in the pages before sin entered the world in Eden. Genesis 1:26–31 explains,

Then God said, "Let us make human beings in our image, to be like us. They will reign over the fish in the sea, the birds in the sky, the livestock, all the wild animals on the earth, and the small animals that scurry along the ground."

> So God created human beings in his own image.
> In the image of God he created them;
> male and female he created them.

> Then God blessed them and said, "Be fruitful
> and multiply. Fill the earth and govern it. Reign over
> the fish in the sea, the birds in the sky, and all the
> animals that scurry along the ground."
> Then God said, "Look! I have given you every
> seed-bearing plant throughout the earth and all
> the fruit trees for your food. And I have given every
> green plant as food for all the wild animals, the
> birds in the sky, and the small animals that scurry
> along the ground—everything that has life." And
> that is what happened.
> Then God looked over all he had made, and he
> saw that it was very good! (NLT)

God scooped up the dirt of the ground and formed a man: "Then the LORD God formed a man from the dust of the ground and breathed into his nostrils the breath of life, and the man became a living being" (Genesis 2:7). This could have been done in such a way that the animated clay that was sculpted to walk, talk, and exist was just like a doll, formed but mindless and obedient only to that which the Creator saw fit Instead, God gave him something greater than mere existence—He gave him life. God breathed His life-breath, spirit-breath into the man so that he could have a mind for himself. A mind that was not a puppet operating in direct command of God, but a mind that could have free will and choice. Now, God in His infinite wisdom knew what giving such a creature this level of freedom would mean just a few verses down the road, but He chose to allow the man to have the gift of his own choice, his own will. The ability to make decisions for himself, and the ability to love God or reject God. What a magnificent and splendor-filled gift.

Then God placed this man in a garden made just for him. "Eden" literally means "delight," and that was exactly what God wanted and intended and desired for man to have. Intimate and direct relationship with the Creator in a garden of paradise to live out all his days. Man disobeyed his Creator and fell into sin, and consequently had to leave the garden, but the heart of God did not change in wanting a garden relationship with us.

Eden was heaven on earth where God and man had fully embraced relationship and had a flawless connection in perfect harmony—until the Fall. Whether man recognizes it or not, the urge to have Eden is what the heart longs for. It is why man gets so fixated on the idea of Utopia. Yet those who do not know God don't see that the only way to have such a place is to be within the Garden of His heart. We can still reclaim the relationship of Eden, but it is in the choice of man today in our own hearts.

Our relationship with God begins the instant we repent and trust in Jesus; then we're born again with His Spirit living in us, giving us communion with Him. Only then can we begin the process of coming to know His character as we grow in our relationship. If you want to get to know God better, get into the Word. John 1:1

explains, "In the beginning was the Word, and the Word was with God, and the Word was God." Talk with God, share your honest heart, feelings, fears, hopes, dreams, and everything in between, but remember to not do all the talking. Invite God to reveal Himself to you in ways that your unique heart can comprehend. Perhaps He will reveal things through a sermon you hear, Scripture verse, or in an unexpected way. Relationship involves communion, and communion involves sitting with Him.

Relationship with God does not mean that instantly every worry, problem, or issue you have is miraculously gone. It does not mean hardships of this world do not come, but it does mean that you no longer walk alone. It also means that you can come into this knowing of the Heart of the One who crafted you. Psalm 139:7–16 says it all:

Where can I go from your Spirit?
    Where can I flee from your presence?
If I go up to the heavens, you are there;
    if I make my bed in the depths, you are there.
If I rise on the wings of the dawn,
    if I settle on the far side of the sea,
even there your hand will guide me,
    your right hand will hold me fast.
If I say, "Surely the darkness will hide me
    and the light become night around me,"
even the darkness will not be dark to you;
    the night will shine like the day,
        for darkness is as light to you.

For you created my inmost being;
>   you knit me together in my mother's womb.
I praise you because I am fearfully and
>   wonderfully made;
>   your works are wonderful,
>   I know that full well.
My frame was not hidden from you
>   when I was made in the secret place,
>   when I was woven together in the depths of
>   the earth.
Your eyes saw my unformed body;
>   all the days ordained for me were written in
>   your book
>   before one of them came to be.

He knew us before we even took our first breaths because He fashioned us in His own image. We bear His image on this earth, His very thumbprint. He has a purpose for every single human being on this planet, and we can come to know what that mission, purpose, and calling is through relationship with Him. It likely won't be revealed overnight, and it may be revealed through doing and action, but if we seek Him, we will find. If we really come to know Him, we will see that He intends to love us, to care for us, and to give us life and life abundantly (John 10:10) through His Son, Jesus Christ, and through His goodness. C. S. Lewis puts it this way:

The terrible thing, the almost impossible thing, is to hand over your whole self—all your wishes and precautions—to Christ. But it is far easier than what we are all trying to do instead. For what we are trying to do is remain what we call "ourselves," to keep personal happiness as our great aim in life, and yet at the same time be "good." We are all trying to let our mind and heart go their own way—centered on money or pleasure or ambition—and hoping, in spite of this, to behave honestly and chastely and humbly.

And that is exactly what Christ warned us you could not do. As He said, a thistle cannot produce figs. If I am a field that contains nothing but grass-seed, I cannot produce wheat. Cutting the grass may keep it short: but I shall still produce grass and no wheat. If I want to produce wheat, the change must go deeper than the surface. I must be plowed up and resown.[10]

Don't underestimate yourself to think that you have no purpose and that you are but a shrub or a random weed on this earth. You are a Wildflower and one that He calls His own creation. Get to know the Gardener and you'll come to know why you are in the garden. Let Him do the work in you that must be done, even if it means you are to be resown, and you will find in the end that you stand as the most magnificent version of yourself that you have ever known.

WHAT YOU BRING TO THE WORLD

The world needs the real you. Not the you that is all packaged up to be easily digested by anyone, not the you that you curate so that others will be pleased, and not the you that you bully yourself into being. The world needs the actual, authentic, absolutely once-in-an-existence Y-O-U.

What you bring to the table is a dish that no one else has ever brought to the potluck of life. Consider how in the span of thousands of years there has never been before and never will be again *you*. Not just in looks, but in your personality, demeanor, ideas, and multi-faceted dynamic aspects. The world has never seen someone quite like you before, and it never will again. It's a seat that only you can fill, and the world needs you.

How cool is it to think that God envisioned the world and all the people and elements it held and felt that it would not be complete unless you were there too? Or how we are so precious to God that our lives as offering to Him are considered to be a sweet aroma (2 Corinthians 2:14). I love the story of Esther as an example of this. Esther was a regular, ordinary girl. In fact, she was Jewish, and at a time when it was not the safest thing to be Jewish in a kingdom that held shifting forms of prejudice and power. Esther had also grown up an orphan, losing her parents at a young age, so she was raised by her uncle. Unbeknown to Esther her future husband was already married, but as with any good story we must stay tuned to find out how it all would play out as to how she becomes his wife and one day Queen.

King Xerxes was not the pretty-boy prince of Disney movies and fairy tales; he was a warrior king who held a firm backbone. His first marriage to Queen Vashti found its way to a dead end and the newly single bachelor king spared no expense in making sure his next wife would not be a mistake like his first one was. In an almost Cinderella-type fashion, all the eligible ladies of the land were invited to come to the palace to see if they would truly be worthy of becoming the next queen. Though she was seemingly just another fish in the sea, Esther stood out among those who knew exactly what the king found most compelling in a woman. For a solid year Esther went through beauty regimens, diet changes, and etiquette training to be ready to even meet this powerful man. When King Xerxes did meet her, he was enthralled by her beauty, her wit, and by what made her exceptionally one-of-a-kind.

As time would tell she became his wife, but her story does not end there. Esther held a vitally important role beyond simply becoming the queen; more than just a role in the kingdom of King Xerxes, she held an important role in the kingdom of God. As Esther's uncle Mordecai stated, "Who knows but that you have come to your royal position for such a time as this?" (Esther 4:14). Take a moment to ponder what that meant for Esther, and what that means for you as well in your own life application.

I seriously doubt Esther thought she would go from an orphaned Jewish girl to queen to the human vessel God used to save the Jewish people. We often have no idea that our existence plays an imperative role not just in the communities where we are presently living, but also in the grander story God has for us in His Story of all of time. As queen, Esther would eventually step in and thwart an attempt to wipe out her people. God had raised her to that exact position because it was her destiny, a role God had hand-picked for her. When you are tempted to believe that your present circumstance is the final destination, don't. I am sure the day before it was announced that the king was looking for a new wife, Esther never dreamed she would one day be living in the palace. The thing about life is we don't know where we are going to end up, so don't assume you know. Instead, recognize and realize that you have a role on this planet and for such a time as this, just as Esther did.

When we consider events like this, we realize that real life is even stranger and more curious than fairy tales, and what a fascinating truth that can be to hold on to. I'm not saying that you are going to be called up to save an entire race and generation of people, but I am also not so naive as to say that can't happen. The future is a beautiful, astounding mystery in the best of ways, and you have an intrinsically unique role in that future.

The world needs who you were purposed and destined to be. If Esther had sabotaged herself and lessened herself to make others feel more comfortable, do you think she would have found herself in the role of queen? If she had talked herself into staying quiet when her people needed her so as to not cause a stir, do you think the Jewish people would have been saved? If Esther had not given her "yes" to God, do you think history would have been different? Consider that the world needed exactly who Esther was, not the person that she probably imagined they wanted. The same is true of you—the world needs you.

The world changers and difference makers are those who no longer deny what they know by conviction to be real, true, and inherently lovely. When you are less concerned with others' opinions, you begin to realize that your focus can be on fulfilling what you were born to do and finding out just exactly what that is. God placed you here in this time for a reason, and that is something only He can reveal to you in His perfect timing through a relationship with Him. If you allow God to have the head seat at your table and approach life with curiosity, He might just take you further than you ever could have even imagined, and there will no longer be the need to pretend to be anything you are not.

PERSONAL REFLECTION
AND APPLICATION QUESTIONS

1. What would an Eden relationship with God look like for you in application?

2. I dare you to ask God why He created you. You might not get the answer right away, but ask. You might be surprised by the answer and the way in which it will be given.

3. What is one way you can grow more in your relationship with God in your current season of life?

4. What does it mean to you personally to be "the fragrance" of God?

CHAPTER 10

Wallflowers Blooming in Real Life

I am not afraid, I was made for this.
—Joan of Arc

However, I consider my life worth nothing to me;
my only aim is to finish the race and complete the task
the Lord Jesus has given me—the task of testifying to the
good news of God's grace.
—Acts 20:24

MY OWN STORY

Perhaps you'd like to know my own Wallflower story, and you may even relate to some of it along the way. I once had someone say to me, "You seem like someone who knows what it's like to be really bullied." At first that felt like a sucker punch to the gut, like I somehow emitted some sort of strange essence like that of a runt-sized bunny with its ear half chewed off. It would take me years to realize that the person who said that did not mean it to be an insult; rather, they recognized within me the spirit of someone who understands firsthand, not just in empathy, what it means to be bullied, ostracized, or left out. That is all very true.

This book was inspired in two ways. The first was a thought that came to me around a decade ago about a Wallflower That Bloomed—a concept that the wallflower didn't have to move to the middle of the room to bloom, or undergo some sort of personality change or makeover to bloom; rather, right where it stood against the wall it had the permission, the opportunity, and the right to bloom. No matter who would gaze upon the wallflower, it bloomed. Regardless of approval, esteem, or praise from anyone else, for it held within the freedom to simply *bloom*. I knew this thought was one given not of my own pondering but was divinely inspired. At the time it seemed too lofty an idea to assume could be said of me, but I held it as a precious phrase awaiting the day when it could be lived out and given to the world to partake in, like one beggar finding bread and sharing it for nourishment with those who also found themselves desperately hungry. The second inspiration came from a conversation I had with the Lord on a prayer walk.

My time spent with God is very sacred and very holy and done in such a way that may not be the norm of most. My intimate time with God is spent in one of two ways for my typical routine, the first being first thing in the morning alongside a cup of coffee. I call it "Coffee with Christ" but really it is enjoying time conversing, complaining, contemplating, or consciously listening to what my Best Friend has to say that day. The other is time spent on a stroll usually through the woods, among trees, or in anything remotely feeling like a forest. God gave me the challenge years ago when I was at the gym to invite Him to walk with me as I physically walked, and from that moment forward I realized He was truly inviting me into something far deeper than just a mere walk. He wanted to walk with me as Adam did in the Garden of Eden in close relationship, in friendship, in Fathering, and beyond. Around the time of my thirtieth birthday, God and I had a very captivating conversation about teenage me, one that left me sitting by a lake crying for many reasons. When you place the blinker on to exit into a new decade, you begin to contemplate the past and the future in full view of your present circumstances.

Together with God I was given a very vivid and clear memory of who I was at thirteen. Thirteen-year-old me was a mixture of myriad facets. She was excessively shy, only willing to speak up in class if called upon, and she was a deep feeler, at times done under by such feelings. Pudgy as many thirteen-year-olds are, she struggled because clothing at the time did not favor pudgy girls. Because plus-sized children's clothing was yet to exist or if it did it was very expensive, my parents found a solid solution in purchasing clothing for me from the husky section for boys in Sears. I didn't mind; jeans were jeans after all, right? The kids at school weren't as kind, and it was hard not being able to fit financially into Limited Too clothing and not be able to fit in the waistline either.

Thirteen-year-old me was also desperate for a friend. I remember hoping so longingly to have girls to invite to my birthday party and hoping this kind blonde girl, Stella, might want to come. But when I went to ask her, our conversation began with her asking my name again. Ouch; even now eighteen years later that one hurts. If having pretty much no friends wasn't enough, the feeling of hardcore rejection from those at Youth Group and Girl Scouts just added to the heaping pile of feeling utterly alone. The girls in my Scout troop all rented a limo to go to the Father-Daughter dance and the girls and parents chose not to even ask if I would like to be included. The mothers told my parents a quick, generic excuse, but it would have been nice if they had at least asked. We weren't that dense either as to pretend there were no other motives and reasons. With how the girls in the troop treated me on a regular basis, it wasn't much of a surprise to me. Then at Youth Group I was purposely left out of invitations to hangouts and such, and even when I got an email to be included on Instant Message, an invitation never arrived. I don't share that to invoke pity for me in you, dear reader, but to instead provide a factual representation of experiences of my adolescence.

Thirteen-year-old me also struggled in that I was a full-on tomboy. It wasn't the boy's husky section clothes that somehow shaped that, it was just a mere fact of life. Softball was one of the greatest joys in my life, and when I wasn't playing or practicing, I was thinking about softball, practicing pitches, or talking about softball with my parents and anyone who would listen. I was a Wallflower in every sense of the word, and it was very emotional to revisit the closet that held those memories from childhood to glimpse thirteen-year-old me. All I wanted to do in those moments was to somehow reach out to that young version of me and hug her. I wanted to reassure her that she was enough, that she didn't need to change to make those around her comfortable, and that she was so very, very worthy.

I wrote this book for any single person, boy or girl, who has ever felt any of the ways I did at thirteen. Because if we base every bit of our worth on the opinions and validation of others, we will never really find the treasure that rests within us to hold so very precious and dear.

My blooming came late in life, and yes, that is a pun. It wasn't one event, and it wasn't something that just occurred overnight. It didn't stop people even now from saying hurtful things or making snide remarks, and it didn't stop me from at times wondering if they are right in saying those things. But nevertheless, my blooming did come over time when I realized that the greatest gift I can ever be in the world is myself. Because there is only one me, and there will only ever be one me.

I spent so many years of my life hoping that if I lost weight I'd be wanted, and once I did, all that met me was an eating disorder to battle and comments that I was now "too skinny." I spent years trying to curate a Frankenstein-type model of myself that would prove lovely to anyone, but the disingenuous feeling within made me want to crawl out of my own skin. There are few things as disgusting and vile as the taste of being a fraud—most especially to oneself.

A day that impacted me was one where I witnessed a young girl being teased the same way I had been. I was working at the Apple Store and was put in charge of helping a Girl Scout Troop coming in for a field trip. I should have known God was up to something in the fact it was a Girl Scout troop, but at the time I didn't even give it a second thought. It was a handful of girls around twelve or thirteen years old coming to the store to learn how to use iPhoto for calendar making. I was helping one young lady with her iPad project when I overheard two of the girls harassing another girl for bringing a Barbie doll along with her to the store. I witnessed the torment done to this quiet little child for no reason whatsoever. I decided to do something about it; it was absolutely awful how they were treating her. I intervened by approaching it from the side. Instead of scolding the two oppressors, I remarked how I adored that the girl had brought her Barbie, sharing that I had one very similar at her age.

Because to this group of girls I was a hip, cool Apple Store instructor, without a beat they changed their tune to be adoring of the doll, not opposed. That moment changed me because I realized two things: one was that we all have the power to help reframe or impact a situation to help the underdog. The second was that if this one little girl was perfectly fine to be who she was, doll and all, then I was valid to do the same as an adult. That one interaction changed the course of my own life.

I'm still a work in progress, a Wallflower in the process of fully blooming, but I am doing, not just considering it anymore. I'm still that thirteen-year-old version of me, and I am at the same instant the thirty-two-year-old version of me. The difference is I am working to continue to heal that thirteen-year-old version of me all while choosing to daily live this thirty-two-year-old version of myself. The obscure music loving, random movie referencing, absolute shenanigan loving, quirky, earthy, adventurer thirty-two-year-old version of Cal.

My life is very alternative in ways because of that choice to live as I was made to be, rather than as one would expect me to be, as a basic millennial easily sorted for a demographic. I am so much more than that, and I live it out. From dressing for my approach rather than my age, from waiting on God to bring about my spouse rather than settling on a quick match, and from authentically stepping out in a million little ways, I don't just walk to the beat of my own drum, I dance. In great and unrestricted freedom, I dance and sing and dream. God told me once I am the Storyteller for the Story Maker, meaning I tell the stories that the Maker of Stories, God, gives me to graciously tell. Instead of rejecting such a title He bestowed upon me with my own feelings of inadequacy or unworthiness, or the fear that using such a title would make me sound cocky like Joseph with his coat of many colors, I now wear it every day with joy. Not with pride or arrogance, but a confident joy because I am who my God says I am, and I am exactly who I was made to be.

My prayer for you, Wallflower, is that you will find through Christ the exuberant and ineffable joy that it is to live abundantly in His presence and live out His call upon your life. You only get one chance to live on this planet, so why not live it in the way that is authentically, fully, fearlessly, and carefully designed to be just for you?

YOUR STORY TO TELL

Knowing exactly how to begin rests in your hands now. Much like entering the ocean, you step in willingly but ready for the sting of the difference. Different is not something bad as we often make it out to be; rather, it is new. And new is not bad; you just are yet to realize how very good it really is to be in the new. Once you've acclimated to the difference, to the new, you'll take another step, and then another. Eventually you'll find yourself so immersed in the ocean of the true you that you'll wonder why it took you so long to get in the water. All it takes is that first step, and then the next one, but a step must be made.

The other side of your fear is freedom. The freedom to be yourself, the freedom to live your life in a way uniquely your own, and the freedom to really live that abundant life—just as God designed for you. Once you have tasted what it means to have the real thing, you will never be able to stomach the counterfeit, and you'll never stand to do it again.

What then will be the story of your blooming? Will it be one of recollection of the former days, ones that held both pain and promise? Will it contain within the tale of a resilient young sapling that endured hurricane-force winds but held on for dear life? Will your story be one where you stopped hiding under a lampshade the Light that you hold that is unlike any the world has ever seen before or will ever see again? Will your story go on to inspire not only those around you, but those yet to even be born? Will your choice to bloom become the legacy of the family tree as a whole? Will you bloom and live to tell the tale? The world needs to hear your story, so much more than you can even fathom.

This all leaves us with the challenge as Wallflowers. We can be the Wallflowers that wilt and waste away collecting dust on the wall, just waiting for the day that we are finally thrown out, or we can bloom exactly where we are in this moment. You don't have to wait until you are moved into that next season or position, you don't have to wait until you think you'll have it all together, and you don't have to wait until you feel accepted or wanted by another human being. You can bloom precisely as you are in this present moment. You are already loved by Someone who died so that you may live; you were made for a purpose and a plan that only the Creator can reveal; and you were destined and designed to live in this very time. You can realize, with the glow of a healthy self-esteem, that you are wonderfully and thoughtfully made, and it is about time that you allow yourself to be the real you. That you give yourself permission to not hide the illustrious light you are under a shade any longer, but you shine the light you were meant to shine. So go onward, courageous one. Go on and bloom because you are worthy, and you are lovely. Stretch out your petals for the world to see just how priceless you are. The world is waiting, so let's see you bloom.

The Wallflower That Bloomed.

PERSONAL REFLECTION
AND APPLICATION QUESTIONS

1. If someone asked you to recount a time when you bloomed instead of wilted, what would that story be? Why would you choose that event or memory?

2. In what area of your life would you like to invite God to help you have more courage to bloom?

3. Who is someone in your life that you would say lives authentically, and what about their life fosters that?

4. Who is someone younger than you who could draw encouragement from a testimony of your own life that you could courageously share?

Notes

1   Ricky Nelson, "Garden Party," Song/ ATV Songs LLC, 1972.

2   Songfacts, "Garden Party" by Rick Nelson <songfacts.com/facts/ rick-nelson/garden-party>

3   Jonathan Foreman, "The Beautiful Letdown," Sparrow Records/ Concord Music Publishing LLC, Capitol CMG Publishing 2004.

4   Debra Michals, "Madam C. J. Walker," National Women's History Museum, 2015 <womenshistory.org/education-resources/ biographies/madam-cj-walker>.

5   "Cast Away" Quotes, IMDb <imdb.com/title/tt0162222/quotes/ ?item=qt0205817>.

6   Ted Camp, "The Story of the Silversmith," October 19, 2017, SilentWord.org <tinyurl.com/35tt9mr3>.

7   Canaan Baca, "More Like Jesus," One Voice INT Music, 2023.

8   "The Tales That Really Mattered…" Tolkien Gateway <tolkiengateway.net/wiki/The_Tales_That_Really_Mattered…>.

9   Erin Gregory and Deborah Courtney, "What Does It Mean To Be Neurodivergent?" *Forbes,* Nov. 10, 2023 <forbes.com/health/mind/ what-is-neurodivergent>.

10 C. S. Lewis, *Mere Christianity* (New York: HarperOne, 1996).

Cally Logan is an author, High School History teacher, and Senior Writer for Crosswalk.com. Her works include *Hang in There, Girl!* and *Dear Future Husband*, which was featured on *The 700 Club Interactive* and *Propel Women*. She mentors college-aged girls and enjoys challenging her students to develop deeper relationships with God and to live authentically and fearlessly. She received her BA Degree from Regent University. In her spare time, she enjoys spending time in nature, woodworking, and watching movies.

"In life, be a snowflake—leave a mark, but no stain."

CallyLogan.com
Instagram: CallyLogan
Twitter/X: CallyLogan